李煜诗词英译全集

COMPLETE COLLECTION OF LI YU'S POETRY

朱曼华 编译

商务印书馆国际有限公司

图书在版编目（CIP）数据

李煜诗词英译全集：英汉对照 / 朱曼华编译 . --
北京：商务印书馆国际有限公司，2017.6
ISBN 978-7-5176-0424-2

Ⅰ . ①李… Ⅱ . ①朱… Ⅲ . ①英语－汉语－对照读物
②词（文学）－作品集－中国－南唐 Ⅳ . ① H319.4：I

中国版本图书馆 CIP 数据核字 (2017) 第 100035 号

Complete Collection of Li Yu's Poetry

李煜诗词英译全集

编　　译　朱曼华
责任编辑　庞洪斌　于　洋
封面设计　蒋宏工作室
出版发行　商务印书馆国际有限公司
地　　址　北京市东城区史家胡同甲 24 号（邮编 100010）
电　　话　010-65592876（总编室）010-65277378（编辑部）
　　　　　010-65598498（市场营销部）
网　　址　www.cpi1993.com
经　　销　全国新华书店
印　　刷　北京中科印刷有限公司
开　　本　710mm × 1000mm　1/16
印　　张　11.5
字　　数　200 千字
版　　次　2017 年 6 月第 1 版第 1 次印刷
书　　号　ISBN 978-7-5176-0424-2
定　　价　30.00 元

序 言

2013年秋，商务印书馆国际有限公司出版了朱曼华学长的译作《中国历代诗词英译集锦》。三年后，他又推出了新的译作《李煜诗词英译全集》，在更高的起点上继续为“中国文化走向世界——影响人类未来”这一伟大文化工程添砖加瓦。

《中国历代诗词英译集锦》出版不久，国家有关部门发来中国对外文化交流译作报表，商务印书馆国际有限公司已将此译作正式上报。该书囊括了朱曼华学长喜爱的、具有一定代表性和广泛性的中国诗词。我曾有机会细读和编辑该书的初稿，对他的译作特色有所了解。而今，他的《李煜诗词英译全集》，是前本译作的姊妹篇，反映了其点面结合的选译思路，体现了其在译介方面的新突破。

李煜在中国词坛上占有十分重要的位置，是当之无愧的“千古词帝”。李煜精书法、工绘画、通音律，诗文均有一定造诣，尤以词的成就最高。其在词上的贡献主要表现在——扩大了词的表现领域，赋予了词更加绚丽的色彩；用情真切，意境深邃，风格独创，别树一帜；语句精练，韵律天成，兼有刚柔之美；具有鲜明的时代性，极富表现力和感染力，给人以特殊的感受，对后世影响深远。

翻译诗词，最重要的是把握原作的神韵和意境。因此在翻译的过程中，既需要对作者、作品的所属时代有所了解，也需要对作者的思想观点、身世际遇、艺术特色和语言风格等有所研究。为了让读者更加深入地了解李煜在诗词方面的造诣，探寻其不同侧面的人生轨迹，朱曼华学长以一己之力，搜集了李煜分散在古典名著中被引用的零星诗句或残句，译介了与李煜诗词相关的史料。其中包括李煜的墓志铭、李煜父皇南唐中主李璟的诗词与南唐先主李昪的诗。此外，对李煜的一些已经无法补齐的残稿或有争议的诗词，译者也一并收入并注明存疑，力求使读者更全面地理解原作，留给读者更宽泛的想象空间。

本书的译文通俗易懂，延续了《中国历代诗词英译集锦》的风格。阅读这本译作，不仅可以全面欣赏李煜的诗词，还有助于从不同角度了解李煜的方方面面。尤其是本书的中英文译注，是解读李煜诗词的重要组成部分，对中国学生通过本书学英文或外国学生学中文具有一定的参考价值。

身为欧美同学会留美分会副会长、副秘书长的朱曼华学长，为《留学生》杂志、《欧美同学会通讯》和欧美同学会网站撰写过大量稿件。在付出辛劳的同时，也历练了笔头。我在欧美同学会工作期间，曾采用过他的多篇来稿，与之结下了笔友之缘。在很长一段时间里，欧美同学会会长的新春祝酒词都是请他英译的，由此了解他是很认真负责的学者。

朱曼华学长在美国留学期间，伊利诺伊大学就发表过他的英文诗。十几年前，他的数首英文诗就曾被美国一家出版社收编，有些还入选了《2005 年最佳诗人和最佳诗作》(*The Best Poets and the Best Poems of 2005*)。因为朱曼华学长一直有用中英文写诗的习惯，有中英文互译的功底，所以他翻译的诗像诗，有味道、有特色，品读起来就像石上的清泉，汩汩而涌，淙淙流淌。

此外，译者一改请名人作序的传统，特邀请我为本书作序。在朱曼华学长译作付梓之际，我不仅向他表示祝贺，更愿意把这本书推荐给欧美同学会的各位学长，推荐给正在学习中文的外国朋友和学习英文的中国朋友，希望大家从中受益。

欧美同学会　李燕朝

【注】“中国文化走向世界——影响人类未来”是朱曼华学长 2001 年秋作为“中西文化交流——许渊冲学术思想和成就研讨会”秘书长受欧美同学会、中国国际文化交流中心、北京大学国际关系学院等会议发起单位委托，起草文件时提出的口号，后来《欧美同学会通讯》等媒体多次用过此提法。

Preface—An Editor's Comment

Autumn in 2013, the Commercial Press International Co., Ltd. published "Chinese Famous Poetry Translated by Manfield Zhu". Three years later, he launched a new translated version as "Complete Collection of Li Yu's Poetry", and continues on a higher starting point to promote "Chinese culture to the world—affect the future of humanity" as a great cultural project.

"Chinese Famous Poetry Translated by Manfield Zhu" published soon, the national authorities sent a document for recording China's external cultural exchange translated works. The Commercial Press International Co., Ltd. was asked to fill in the recorded-table with Zhu's translated works to submit to the authority. "Chinese Famous Poetry Translated by Manfield Zhu" includes almost Zhu's favorite Chinese poems that could represent outstanding achievements of classic and modern Chinese poetry. I had the opportunity to peruse the manuscript of the book, and I began to understand his translation style. Now, "Complete Collection of Li Yu's Poetry" can be considered as a companion piece, reflecting his philosophical idea that the general should be combined with the special. Such an idea used to explain why he wanted to translate Emperor Li Yu's poetry.

Li Yu occupied a very important position in the Chinese Ci poetry, being worthy of "eternal the Chinese Ci poetry emperor". Li Yu was good in calligraphy, painting work and rhyme or rhythm. He was talented both in poetry and essay he could write skillfully, especially with the highest achievements in the Chinese Ci poetry. He was mainly to expand the Chinese Ci poetry performance field with his exceptional style, upholding his unique banner to express his pure feelings and profound artistic conception, with both hard and soft beauty; his poetic words seem natural with refining generalization, natural rhythm, expressive force and appeal; with distinct time features. And particularity, his Chinese Ci poetry has had profound impact on later generations.

As for translation of poetry, the most important thing is to grasp the meaning charm, grasp the original poem's emotional mood. Therefore, in the translation process, it is not only necessary to understand the poet with his works' era, but also necessary to understand the poet's ideas, life experience encounters, artistic features and language style by means of study. In order to make the world a deeper understanding of the characteristics of Li Yu's attainments in poetry, the translator has explored different aspects of the poet's life trajectory for showing Li Yu's brilliant artistic achievements. Manfield Zhu was single-handedly to collect the scattered verse or sentence residues dispersed in the classic works. He not only translated all the emperor's poems or Ci poems, but also translated Li Yu's epitaph as well as all of his father's and grandfather's poetry. Some of Li Yu's poetic residues have been unable to recognize their original manuscripts, and others may be controversial to make sure whether they were Li Lu's poetry or not. Anyway the translator tried to collect them and make annotations for reference. Doing so aims at leaving readers' imagination space.

Thus, reading this book, not only you can fully appreciate the poetry of Li Yu, but also you can understand all aspects from different angles. Especially Chinese-English annotations of the book are also an important part for understanding Li Yu with his poems. It is helpful for Chinese students to have certain reference value through the book to learn English or foreign students to learn Chinese.

Over the years, as deputy secretary-general, and vice president of American Alumni of WRSA, Manfield Zhu wrote numerous articles to mail to the magazine "Abroad-Studying Students", "Western Returned Scholars Association Newsletter", and WRSA website. Paying hard work, he also accumulated the experience of his writing. I used to work at the Western Returned Scholars Association; I had used his many papers. He has been one of the best pen pals.

For a long period of time, it is he who must be asked to translate the WRSA president's Chinese New Year Toasts for many past years. Thus I understand that he is a very serious, very responsible scholar.

Thirty years ago, as a visiting scholar, Manfield Zhu studied English in the United States, and began to write poems in English, one of which was published in the ILLINI

WEEK of University of Illinois. Ten years ago, some of his English poems were selected and published by a US publishing house. Some were selected and compiled into an American anthology of poetry entitled the <*The Best Poets and the Best Poems of 2005*>. Because he has been having a useful habit of writing poetry in English, and has a good grounding in English translation, so his translated poems are like poetry. His translated poems read usually to be fluent, tasteful, and distinctive, like gurgling springs flowing, like stream washing riverbed stone, trickling.

His translation is easy to read and understand, which continues to keep the style of "Chinese Famous Poetry Translated by Manfield Zhu".

Usually, an author or a translator would like to invite a well-known scholar to write a preface or foreword, however, Manfield Zhu asked me to write a few words as a preface to his newly translated works, which reflects his pragmatic attitude toward research. This spring, Manfield Zhu would like to have his newly-translated works published, let me not only bless him and recommend this book to every member of the Western Returned Scholars Association, but also recommend to foreign friends who are learning Chinese and recommend Chinese students to learn English with the help of such a newly-translated works. I hope everyone will benefit much from it a lot.

Yanchao Lee,
The Western Returned Scholars Association

[Note] "Chinese culture to enter the world—affect the future of humanity" was used as a slogan of an academic symposium— "Cultural Communication—Xu Yuanchong Academic Thought and Achievement Seminar" in fall of 2001 at Peking University. Manfield Zhu was selected as the Secretary-General of the symposium in which for the first time he mentioned such an idea to emphasize it was important for the Chinese translators to introduce Chinese culture to the world. On behalf of Western Returned Scholars Association,

China International Cultural Exchange Center, Beijing University Institute of International Relations and all the conference-sponsored units, Manfield Zhu was commissioned to report the symposium initially by using such a slogan.

自 序

去年深秋，我开始英译《李煜诗词英译全集》，历时八个月完成了设定的目标。在江南自家的“姑苏台”上，无酒对月，有茶相伴，寂寞但不孤独。译完南唐后主所有能收集到的诗词（包括一些残句），译兴丝毫未减，又英译了其父皇李璟（南唐中主）、祖父李昪（南唐先主）的诗词。同时英译了南唐朝臣徐铉给李煜撰写的墓志铭。把李煜的墓志铭和李昪、李璟诗词作为附录有助于读者系统地解读千古词帝李煜。李煜在诗词方面所取得的成就高山仰止。2013年秋，商务印书馆国际有限公司出版了我的译作《中国历代诗词英译集锦》。该书从选译比《诗经》还早的无名氏的《击壤歌》到唐诗宋词元曲，直至陈晓旭的《黛玉》等新诗，共英译了234首诗词，大体上涵盖了中国各个历史阶段有一定代表性的诗词。这次英译李煜诗词全集，旨在深入解读历史人物的艺术特色，传播其作品的艺术成就；旨在淡化以往的传统观念，重新认识李后主的历史价值和人格魅力。英译李煜诗词全集，是译者对李煜作品的再学习再解读的过程。集结、梳理、翻译更多的能找寻到的李煜作品，给中外读者更多认识理解李煜的途径，远比只在读者熟悉的几篇诗词上做文章更有意义。

南唐时期，盛唐及其诗歌已经走完了灿烂光辉的历程。晚唐就如最后一抹残阳，送走了留不住的黄昏。此时只有李煜这位善写诗词的帝王，如深夜晴空的星辰熠熠生辉，为中国长天的夜色添彩。他以天与地之间的孤独，以无可言说的落寞，以亘古未有的君王感悟，绚烂并丰富了人类的情感世界。在唐以后的一段历史时期中，诗与词是有分工的。从习惯上看，通常是欢快时喜欢填词，悲痛时则喜欢写诗。李煜虽被冠以“千古词帝”，但仍不可小视他的诗作。《昭惠周后诔》是李煜传世最长的一篇挽诗，共246行，1313字，其行数为白居易《长恨歌》两倍还多，字数比840字的《长恨歌》还多出473个字。该诗是悼念娥皇大周后的辞世之作，情真意切，动人心弦，堪称南唐佳作。该诗把娥皇的天生丽质、才高貌美、能歌善舞描写得淋漓尽致，更把娥皇仙逝所引起的悲痛，写得撕心裂肺，对送葬礼仪的庄严肃穆，对如游龙般的灵车行进等诸多细节的描绘，都给读者留下了深刻的印象。

李煜在挽辞中说娥皇是

“纤眉范月

高髻凌风”

仅仅八个字，就把美人眉清目秀的形象和美丽的发式栩栩如生地画在了纸上。长期以来，人们的注意力只在李煜的《虞美人》《相见欢》《浪淘沙》等脍炙人口的几首词上，对更能反映李煜感情世界的这篇长诗似乎有所忽略。仔细研究原文，读者会发现李煜非常熟悉历史，他是认真博览群书的皇帝，是挥笔自如、才高八斗的文豪。李煜短暂的一生，留下的不只是他令人百读不厌、千古绝美的行行诗词，更重要的是他那真实、丰富的情感世界。他在娥皇的琴背上、扇面上、手帕上，在柳叶上，灵车上等情感所及之处，都留有不朽的诗句。他的作品饱含了似水柔情。

李煜的《破阵子》一词，大体上概括了他一生的坎坷：

四十年来家国，

三千里地山河。

凤阁龙楼连霄汉，

玉树琼枝作烟萝。

几曾识干戈？

一旦归为臣虏，

沈腰潘鬓消磨。

最是仓皇辞庙日，

教坊犹奏别离歌。

垂泪对宫娥。

即便丢了江山，李煜也不会忘记对美人倾诉。

清代诗人赵翼有首《题遗山诗》：

身阅兴亡浩劫空，两朝文献一衰翁。

无官未害餐周粟，有史深愁失楚弓。

行殿幽兰悲夜火，故都乔木泣秋风。

国家不幸诗家幸，赋到沧桑句便工。

到了五代十国时期，盛唐的辉煌已成为过去，企盼唐的后裔有回天之力，重演贞观之治的盛景，只能是一枕黄粱。李煜面对当时的强权，被迫走上归顺之路，也是一种无奈的选择。如果从帝相的角度评价李煜，诗人赵翼的结论是比较客观的。如果以更广阔的视野分析，一位帝王能留下这样多彩的文学遗产，已经很对得起祖先和后人了。即便成为阶下囚，李煜仍然保持南唐的气节和风骨。他守住了做人的底线，他的情操，他的童真，他杰出的诗词成就，为他赢得了“千古词帝”的美誉。英译李煜诗词全集所遇到的困难，首先是如何确切地把握李煜所处的时代脉搏和对他所使用的诗词语言的准确理解。数月的英译实践，收到了“以译促学，以学带译”的实效。希望本书的英译，能再现李煜诗词的真实风貌。

译者坚持2013年秋出版的《中国历代诗词英译集锦》的英译风格——译诗像诗，神貌结合，大体押韵，有节奏感，通俗上口。本书译者注重译文形象和意境的再创造，注意以英语为母语的读者对译文的反馈。希望译文能给读者以更多的想象空间。希望本书成为中国人学英文、外国人学中文的通俗读物，成为深入解读李煜及其诗词的参考用书。

中英文注释或译注，是本书的重要组成部分，译注为解读李煜诗词提供了翔实的资料。中文译注对学中文的中外学生尤为宝贵，可节约读者大量查阅工具书的时间。本书中英文译注不是逐一对应的，内容亦不尽相同。因为英文译文在很大程度上已经为解读原文打下了基础，有些地方不需要重复注释。李煜诗词流行的版本很多，一直以来都有一些存疑问题。在李煜全集或选集中，也发现过明显的文字错误，如“矢”“失”相混等。本书通过译注，对一些存疑问题尽可能地给出清楚的交代。公元978年李煜谢世后，宋元明清各代对李煜和李煜诗词的关注有增无减。李煜很多失传了的诗词，在一些涉及李煜的著作中已经陆续发现。本书辑录的李煜的残句，主要就是在文人墨客的行文中发现的。可以找到李煜诗词线索的著作很多，如陆游《老学庵笔记》，叶梦得（1077~1148）《石林燕语》，元代方回(1227 ~ 1306)《瀛奎律髓注》，《翰府名谈》，《野客丛谈》，《海录碎事》，《孔帖》等，对读者深入解读李煜的作品很有帮助。

令人兴奋的是，在当代网络世界中，一大批国内外学者成了李煜的新粉丝。每年一到李煜生日——七夕，就有声势浩大的自发性笔会。届时会有大批高质量的文章出现，高度赞美歌颂李煜对中国传统文化的杰出贡献。在一次网络“七夕晚祭李煜文会”上，一位叫“渌水忆兰”的核心会员写了《七夕祭后主》等诗文，令人感慨万千。现仅摘录些许片段，供读者欣赏：

“……步步生莲的女子，写尽自己一生的痛，只为舞一曲绝世的美博你欢颜。红尘如许，红颜美眷相伴相惜，你终究是个有福之人，只无奈林花谢春红，太匆匆，醉时欢歌的一场繁梦只如烟花一瞬，而如今，故国不堪回首，明月虽在，也异当时，凄清照鬓丝。众人皆说，你醉心诗词歌赋，错生于帝王之家，可我始终觉得，你这一生是历史的选择。山河破碎，承载你半世和泪和血的伤痛，身世浮沉，却成就你千古词帝的光辉……”

已经由商务印书馆国际有限公司于2013年出版的《中国历代诗词英译集锦》和这本书的初稿都曾得到过石凡的许多具体指导与帮助。愿借此机会向她表示最诚挚的敬意和谢意。

朱曼华

Translator's Preamble

Last late autumn, I started to translate "Complete Collection of Li Yu's Poetry". Doing off and on, it has lasted for eight months to complete the English version. On my own Suzhou Dew Pavilion of Building Top, I had no cup of wine to dedicate to the moon but had tea drinks as my partner, therefore I am not lonely.

Completing all of Li Yu's poems or ci poems, including some of his incomplete residual poems, either phrases or sentences, still I felt energetic to do more, therefore, also I had to translate his father's and his grandfather's poems in all. Moreover, I translated Li Yu's epitaph that comprehensively summed up his whole life and experience. It's his imperial official Xu Xuan who was told to write such a biographical works. The translator gave a brief introduction to the South Tang as an appendix. The poetry written by Li Yu's elder generations could be used to tell readers the fact that Li Yu came from a scholarly family, and that Li Yu's achievements were not isolated from his family surroundings. In autumn, 2013, the Commercial Press International Co., Ltd. published my "Chinese Famous Poetry Translated by Manfield Zhu", in which 234 classical and modern poems were translated into English, including the Chinese earliest folk songs, Tang poems, Song ci poems, Yuan qu poems and the newest poems, which could represent the achievements of Chinese Poetry Kingdom. This time the translator would like to translate Li Yu's all the poems and ci poems in order to dilute any class bias or specious traditional ideas, and to reinterpret the South Tang artistic achievements and characteristics, and re-estimate Li Yu's historical poetic value. "Writing mirrors the writer" or "Style is the man". Only reading and understanding Li Yu's complete works could help us truly get familiar with his inner world. Doing so meant to seek for more scientific, objective research on his complete works rather than just depending of his limited few well-known poems and ci poems. History can not be considered as arbitrarily rubbing dough; history must be respected and objectively written. The historian must be a truth-seeking man to restore the historical figures as it is. The South Tang entered a turning point in Chinese history, Tang and his poetry had reached the highest splendor of history, but the Late Tang seemed to be a faint evening sun with the last residual rosy cloud. In such an evening, only one emperor like a bright star glittering at dark night continued to sparkle, to add luster to China's long sky in darkness. It is he that still continued to beautify China with real human feelings in the world. In the historical period after the Tang Dynasty, the poetry and ci poetry seemed to still have a functional division, usually, when there was something happy, a metrical poem would be written whereas something sad happened, a ci poem would be used so as to fit the whole atmosphere. Although Li Yu was known as the "Eternal Ci Poetry Emperor", but still he wrote quite a lot of common metrical poetry instead of so-called ci poetry. "Eulogy to Queen Zhaohui Zhou" was a long elegy consisting of 1313 Chinese characters with 246 lines of poetry, which is longer than poet Bai Juyi's long poem Eternal Grief in length. Li Yu's long poem was for the mourning after Queen Ehuang's death. Such an elegy was so affectionate, so excitable that could be called the South-Tang eternal masterpiece. The poem highly praised Ehuang to be natural in beauty, versatile in talent and good at singing and dancing. The long elegy vividly reappeared the grief caused by Ehuang passing away, vividly described the solemn ritual of the funeral in detail that left readers a very deep impression. Li Yu's elegy was full of truly lingering love.

In his long elegy, Li Yu depicted his Queen Ehuang like this:

"Your slender brows simulating the crescent,

Your bun by wind blowing reached top height."

Only eight Chinese characters used to depict Queen Ehuang, readers could find her dignified and generous external image like a beautiful painting. For a long time, people's attention were only paid to Li Yu's few of poems, such as <Beautiful-Lady-Yu>,<Joyful Reunion>,<Billows Washing Sands>,etc. His other metrical long poem, such as <Eulogy to Queen Zhaohui> has been neglected though it was much better to reflect his true feelings of inner world. Translating "Complete Collection of Li Yu's Poetry" for the translator fundamentally means relearning and reinterpreting Li Yu's works. It is inevitable for the translator to take more careful consideration of Li Lu's original works, it is easy to find that Li Yu was more familiar with Chinese historical figures or events. His mind was full of historical stories or anecdotes. He was really a good-reading emperor in history. Really he had read myriad copies of classical books. He was not skilful at applying his sword, but he was absolutely good at writing poems or ci poems with his Chinese brush. At age of 42, Li Yu ended his short life but left us not only his everlasting poetry but also his truly rich affectionate inner world, which is more important than anything else. He wrote poems on Ehuang's violin back side, on her silk fan, her handkerchief, and on the weeping willow leaf and on her hearse, etc. All his poetic lines or words were so emotional and immortal. He was never like a majestic emperor, but just like a supreme wise man as appropriate as a sweetheart. Of course, he also had masculine beauty, and made a loud rough cry sometimes, but in general, he was as gentle as watery tenderness.

<Breakthrough Battle Array> written by Li Yu comprehensively summed up the fate of the ups and downs of his life:

It's my homeland with forty-year history,

With 3000-km mountain-and-river territory.

Dragon-phoenix style pavilions link with the Milky Way,

Jadelike trees with everlasting long twigs seem misty.

Fighting by sword never suited my character!

Yet once got as an official captive member,

He would turn lean, haggard with gray hair.

It's extremely farewell to ancestral temple,

Imperial musicians played a song of farewell.

Tears dropped toward maidens of the palace hall.

Lost his country, Li Yu also did not forget to tell his mind to his imperial beautiful maidens.

The Qing Dynasty poet Zhao Yi wrote a poem entitled "Inscription to Poet Yishan" as follows:

Seeing the Holocaust disorderly rise and fall,

Two dynasties documents you collected in all.

No official title, no need to seek for others' bestow,

Afraid of losing Chu bow was a historical sorrow.

Orchid's row seemed to be sad of night fire burnt,

The ancient capital lofty trees wept for autumn wind.

With national unfortunate, a poet had good luck,

The vicissitudes made him write the best work.

In China's Five Dynasties of Ten Kingdoms historical period, Tang's glorious page of history had passed, hoping its descendants would restore and repeat its Golden Years of history can only be a daydream. Facing the Song-Dynasty strong power, Li Yu met serious frustration, being captured, he selected a realistic way, which should not be criticized. Only according to an emperor's personal gain or loss, to estimate him, we would like to appreciate poet Zhao Yi's conclusions that should be beyond reproach. But if in a broader perspective or point of view, we also do not have to expect much more achievements in his reign period. Thousands of years of history told us that it was the time situation would basically decide a hero or an emperor's fate. If an emperor could develop his strong points and avoid his weak points so as to leave precious legacy to later generations, then it would be worthy of it by their ancestors and descendants to be proud of him. To this end, it should be no timid to say that during China's thousands of years, only one emperor's poetry or ci poetry was the best, which should be the pride of the Chinese nation. Even though he became a prisoner under the Song Dynasty palace's stone steps, he still remained of his own South Tang integrity and strength of character. He loved the common people as if loving his own son. He kept on sticking to his Buddhist faith considered as for his own bottom line in life. It was not easy for him to maintain his sentiments, his childhood purity, and his outstanding poetry achievements created by such an Eternal Ci Poetry Emperor—His imperial life was short, but his poetic life would be eternal. The main difficulties I have encountered first is how exactly to grasp the historical or social pulse hidden in Li Yu's poems that need an accurate understanding. Translation practice for eight months has won better results to interpret and promote my own learning from translation. Still I hope my translation works will reproduce the real life style thousands of years ago as if Li Yu were writing his poetry just yesterday. The translator has still insisted his own translation principle and style, which is similar with his published "Chinese Famous Poetry Translated by Manfield Zhu" published by the Commercial Press International Co., Ltd. in autumn 2013, Beijing, China. "The translated poem is still as similar as the original poem in meaning and in form, even in rhythm and rhyme read fluently". The translator attached great importance to recreating the image or the mood of the original poetry. The translator considered English native speakers' feedback as the most important principle of translation.

Hope my translation in English both with Chinese annotation and English annotation will give readers more room for imagination.

Hope this book will become a voiceless teacher and true friend of all the students and young teachers who are studying Chinese or English in self-study way.

Hope this book also can be used for reinterpret Li Yu poetry reference.

Annotation in Chinese writing or in English is an important part of this book. "Annotation" for the interpretation of Li Yu poetry provides a wealth of informative and reliable information. Among them, Annotation in Chinese can help learning Chinese, which can save foreign students plenty of time to examine dictionaries, so it is particularly valuable for the Chinese-learning foreign students. Annotation in Chinese is not exactly the same with Annotation in English. Because the English translation has been largely laid the foundation for the interpretation of the original, it is no longer necessary to repeat some explanations. In many popular versions of Li Yu poetry, there exists the so-called "true or false" problem. Some poetry were not written by Li Yu but considered as Li Yu's. At the same time, both Li Yu's complete works and anthologies are often to be found some writing or spelling errors in original text. For example, " 失 "(lost) is mistaken for " 矢 "(vector). More similar mistakes like this are easily seen in different version of Li Yu's Works. My "Annotation" as an appendix to each Li Lu's poem could be used to correct writing or spelling mistakes by means of clear explanations. In 978 AD, Li Yu passed away. The later dynasties, Song, Yuan, Ming and Qing Dynasties kept on attention to his poetry carefully and enthusiastically. More and more people were increasingly interested in his poetry. Li Yu lost a lot of his own poems, some of which have been and will continue to be found with the help of new information or message on Li Yu's relics, including folk stories or anecdotes. Some residual poetic sentences are mainly found in the classic works by well-known writers or experts. Nowadays more and more clues on Emperor Li Yu's writings have been found in some classic works, such as "Annotation in Old School Hut", "Swallow-Speech in Stone Forest", "Annotations on Tang-Song Best Lyric Anthology","Imperial Academy Famous Sayings","Seclusion Literati Conversations","Widely-recorded unsystematic matters", and "Confucian-compiled Anthology of Classic Works", etc., from which Li Yu's poetry-related records and meaningful interpretations that must be helpful to all the readers who want to master Chinese and English both at home and abroad. It is excited that a large number of domestic and foreign students have become new poetic fans of Li Yu whenever his birthday is to come—July 7th, Tanabata, each year, there must be a celebration activity on Li Yu in contemporary online world, and there will be one great spontaneous pen-pals-meeting when a large number of high-quality poetry to be published, highly to praise Li Yu's outstanding contribution to Chinese traditional culture. In a network, "Tanabata Festival of Li Yu Literature and Art" was once held. A pen pal called "Lushuiyilan" as a key member of Pen Pals wrote "Tanabata Festival Recalling Emperor Li Yu" and other poems, filled with emotion.

Excerpts: only a little fragments here for readers to enjoy:

"A lotuslike girl was walking on her gentle feet, step by step, as if a lotus flower were blooming with her each step. She has written all of her pain in her whole life just in order to dance beautifully to let you smile. You tried your best to do whatever you like in your own kingdom; and eventually you were considered as a happy man for you have had a beautiful queen accompanying you. However, no one could prevent spring flowers from falling down, which seemed to be blooming in too short time, just like a tipsy man's short dream, and just like fireworks shining a moment.

Nowadays it is painful for you to look back to your homeland though the moon is still bright, but it is quite different from the original moon hovering over your palace and your sideburns. All the people say that you were just intoxicated in poetry, different kinds of poetry, and that you were born in an imperial family is not your own mistake. Eventually I think that's a history choice. Your homeland lost, you were heartbroken to shed your tears, but you never changed your mind to love your country. No matter whatever happened to it, rise or fall, it has established your eternal poet's glory."

In the process of my English translation, Senior Editor Stone Fan has always been concerned about my understanding the inside meaning of each poem or ci poem. She often gives me effective help and guidance in detail. Let me take this opportunity to express my best wishes and heartfelt thanks to her.

Manfield Zhu

目 录

第一部分 诗
Part One Poems

第二部分　词
Part Two Ci Poems

第三部分
Part Three
（一）英译南唐中主李璟诗词全集（7首）
（二）英译南唐先主李昪唯一传世之诗

附　录

第一部分　诗

Part One Poems

秋莺

残莺何事不知秋，
横过幽林尚独游。
老舌百般倾耳听，
深黄一点入烟流。
栖迟背世同悲鲁①，
浏亮②如笙碎在缑③。
莫更留连好归去，
露华凄冷蓼花④愁。

【译注】

①从前有一只海鸟停留在鲁国国都的郊外，鲁侯让人驾车迎接它，并且在宗庙里对它敬酒、赐美食又奏乐使它高兴，但海鸟眼睛昏花，看不清楚，忧愁悲伤，不吃不喝，三天后就死了。这典故讥讽用别人供养自己的方式来养鸟，不是养鸟是害鸟。

②浏亮：亦作浏湸，清楚明朗。

③缑（gōu）：即缑氏山（在河南偃师）。周灵王太子晋，王子乔也，好吹笙，作凤凰鸣。曾游此山。三十余年后，又求之于山上，至时，果乘白鹤驻山头，修道成仙。

④蓼花：Polygonum hydropiper 草本植物，穗状花序。花絮似雪，穗若串珠。

Autumn Oriole

What made an oriole not know autumn coming?
Why the bird crossed the forest to travel alone?
Time and again it kept singing a song in an old tone,
Like a yellow dot, it disappeared into the mist soon.
It settled down late not to suit the nature of Lu* local,
Like Prince Jin** playing flute to release his sorrow.
Don't be reluctant to leave here and far to go,
Polygonum flowers are sad with the bleak dew.

[Annotation]

* Lu here refers to an ancient Kingdom Lu (today's Shandong Province, China).

** Prince Jin's story happened in the ancient Zhou Dynasty, China.

病起题山舍壁

山舍初成病乍轻，
杖藜巾褐称闲情。
炉开小火深回暖，
沟引新流几曲声。
暂约彭涓①安朽质，
终期宗远②问无生。
谁能役役③尘中累，
贪合鱼龙构强名。

【译注】

①彭涓：彭祖和涓子并称，二人均为传说中的长寿者。传说彭祖姓篯名铿，颛顼玄孙，生于夏代，至殷末时已七百六十七岁（一说八百余岁）。又据《楚辞·天问》："彭铿斟雉帝何乡食，受寿永多夫何久长。"王逸注谓彭祖善调雉羹以事帝尧，被尧所赞美。

②宗远：宗炳和慧远。宗炳（375—443），南朝（宋）高僧、画家；慧远（334—416），俗姓贾，南朝高僧，中观般若学大师，弘扬西方净土法门，被尊为净土宗初祖。

③役役：劳苦不息貌。《庄子·齐物论》："终身役役，而不见其成功。"

A Poem Inscribed on the Cliff Wall

The hilly villa was just built, my illness abruptly lighter,
A walking stick and a brown scarf showed idle delight.
Oven small fire warmed my villa deeply,
A fresh creek was singing songs out of gully.
I associated my illness with Longevity God Peng and Juan,
Still I would ask a question to Eminent Monk Zong or Yuan.
In the human world, working hard, everybody is busy,
In order to get fame or preys, each one must be greedy.

送邓王二十弟从益牧[1]宣城[2]

且[3]维轻舸更迟迟，
别酒重倾惜解携[4]。
浩浪侵愁光荡漾，
乱山凝恨[5]色高低。
君驰桧楫[6]情何极，
我凭阑干日向西。
咫尺烟江几多地，
不须怀抱重凄凄。

Send off My Younger Brother to Take up Office

Reluctantly to start a small boat to slowly sail,
Let us drink more cups of wine for farewell.
Sparkling waves were rippling with much sorrow,
Coagulating hates, colorful mountains high or low.
How extremely energetically you are to paddle,
I lean upon balustrade to see the setting sun low.
The misty river is just at a stone's throw,
Do not feel desolate with much sorrow.

【译注】

①牧：古时用其管理、统治之意。州官即州牧。本诗是李煜在金陵送胞弟邓王李从益赴宣城任职时所作。收尾句流露出李煜宽慰弟弟之情，希望他乐观豁达，亦兼有鞭策之意，劝勉弟弟不宜腹藏离愁别恨，要以国事为重。

②宣城：位于安徽东南部，与江苏、浙江两省接壤，是东南沿海沟通内地的重要通道。处在沪宁杭大三角的西部腰线上，是中部地区承接东部地区产业和资本转移的前沿阵地。

③且：暂且；姑且。

④解携：分手，离别。

⑤乱山凝恨：孤帆远影已不见，只有那高高低低的山色峰峦映入眼帘，仿佛凝结着许多遗恨。诗人移情于景，含蓄地表达了自己的离愁别恨。

⑥桧楫（guì jí）：桧木做的船桨。

悼诗[1]

永念难消释，
孤怀痛自嗟[2]。
雨深秋寂莫，
愁引病增加。
咽绝[3]风前思，
昏蒙[4]眼上花。
空王[5]应念我，
穷子正迷家。

Mourning Poem

To release eternal memories of my child is not easy,
Alone I am still lamented for him passing away.
The rain deepened the lonely autumn,
The sorrow let me ill seriously again.
A sore throat will never be to fit the breeze,
The twilight must blur eyes to see flowers.
Buddha King should concern me cordially,
My pitiful kid was losing his home way.

【译注】

①《全唐诗》卷 8-11 第 114 首。
②嗟（jiē）：叹息。（沉浸在丧子的巨大悲痛中，当时娥皇正病重，李煜还不想告诉她，只有自己承受这种痛。当时南唐江山风雨飘摇，也正在受到北宋的威胁。）
③咽绝：呼吸困难，咽喉肿痛。
④蒙：同“濛”，遮盖。
⑤空王：对佛的尊称。佛家以为世界皆空。

挽辞①（二首）

其一

珠碎眼前珍，
花凋世外春。
未销心里恨，
又失掌中身。
玉笥②犹残药，
香奁③已染尘。
前哀将后感，
无泪可沾巾。

【译注】

①李煜《挽辞》为其次子仲宣及娥皇大周后谢世所作。

②笥（sì）：器皿，竹器。

③奁（lián）：古代盛梳妆用品的匣子。

Elegy（1~2）

One

In front of my eyes, my pearl has been broken,
In this spring world, a flower is no longer open.
A sad regret still hidden in my heart bottom,
Another favorite pearl being lost in my palm.
Her jade box still having the residual medicine,
Her fragrant mirror has been full of dust again.
The former sadness turned my later mourning,
No shedding tears wet my mourning clothing.

其二

艳质同芳树，
浮危[1]道略同。
正悲春落实，
又苦雨伤丛。
秾丽[2]今何在，
飘零事已空。
沉沉[3]无问处，
千载谢东风。

Two

Her good morality was like a fragrant tree,
Growing up in turbulence, in disorderly way.
In grieving of spring fruit falling on ground,
I worry the rain to injure the trees in wound.
Where is to seek for such a beauty?
Everything is gone to be empty.
There is no place to ask "where is she?",
I would thank the east wind for helping me.

【译注】

①浮危：动荡危险。
②秾（nóng）丽：艳丽。
③沉沉：沉重，深沉。

感怀①（二首）

其一

又见桐花②发旧枝，
一楼烟雨暮凄凄。
凭阑惆怅人谁会，
不觉潸然泪眼低。

其二

层城无复见娇姿，
佳节缠哀不自持。
空有当年旧烟月，
芙蓉城上哭蛾眉③。

【译注】

①古代帝王后宫佳丽三千，能将其心思专注在一个后妃身上的，又不变迁其爱情者，几乎只有李煜一位。他对亡妻娥皇所表现出的诚挚爱意，在历代帝王中绝无仅有。

② 桐花：（Tung flower / blossom, Aegiceras corniculatum）清明"节气"之花，是自然时序的物候标记；三春之景到清明绚烂至极致，但同时盈虚有数、由盛转衰。桐花因此而成为两种悖反意趣的承载。政治仪式、宴乐游春、祭祀思念等社会习俗构成了桐花意象的文化内涵。中唐时期，桐花"自开还自落""纷纷开且落"与诗人的落寞寡合。

③蛾眉：也作娥眉，指女子细长的眉毛，泛指貌美的女子。

My Lovesick Memories（1~2）

One

Memorial blossoms out of old twigs were seen again,
The misty twilight shrouded a lonely pavilion in rain.
Leaning upon the balustrade, I am melancholy to whom?
I cannot help shedding tears abruptly from heart bottom.

Two

On watchtower, your charming was no longer seen,
On happy holiday, I could not bear my lovesick pain.
My mind was empty only with the misty ancient moon,
On the Lotus-City Wall, I wept for my dear queen.

梅花（二首）

其一

殷勤[1]移植地[2]，
曲槛[3]小栏边。
共约重芳日，
还忧不盛妍[4]。
阻风开步障[5]，
乘月溉寒泉。
谁料花前后，
蛾眉[6]却不全。

Plum in Bloom

One

Sincerely we planted plum in the garden site,
The railing winding around flowery bed side.
We predicted whether they would survive,
Unable to make sure they would be alive.
Set up the screen to prevent the wind from blowing,
To ride on the moon to irrigate plum by cold spring.
Who can tell when the planted plum will open?
As my queen passed away to the west heaven.

【译注】

①殷勤：情意恳切深厚。司马迁《报任少卿书》："未尝衔杯酒，接殷勤之欢。"

②据《全唐诗》载："后主尝与周后移植梅花于瑶光殿之西，及花时，而后已殂，因成诗见意。"

③槛（jiàn）：（窗户或门廊或水井边的）栏杆。

④妍（yán）：美。李白《于阗采花》诗："丹青能令丑者妍。"

⑤步障：遮蔽风尘或视线的一种屏幕。

⑥蛾眉：女子长而美的眉毛。常作美女的代称。这里指大周后娥皇。

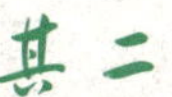

其二

失却烟花主，
东君[1]自不知。
清香更何用，
犹发去年枝。

Two

I lost my misty flowery princess,
The sun did not know my loss.
The spring fragrance has been useless,
It originated from last plum sprigs.

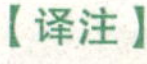

【译注】

①东君：太阳神名，亦指太阳。

书灵筵手巾

浮生共憔悴，
壮岁失婵娟。
汗手遗香渍，
痕眉染黛烟。

Elegy Written on Her Coffin Label

We were sharing a mutual haggard life,
In the prime life, I lost my beautiful love.
Sweat hands' fragrance still in handkerchief,
Each eyebrow turned into a black-dyed leaf.

【译注】

此五言绝句是李煜怀念亡后娥皇之作。

书琵琶背

侁自肩如削，
难胜数缕绦。
天香留凤尾，
馀暖在檀槽。

【译注】

《书琵琶背》实为李煜写给昭惠周后的挽诗。睹物思人，作者借初逢时赠给娥皇的琵琶寄托哀思，无限感慨，从琵琶各个侧面反复渲染，淋漓尽致地展现了他内心世界的痛苦，表达了自己凄苦寂寞之情。这诗真实地记载了妻亡子夭的悲苦，而在他的词里却很少直接反映这段生活经历。这类诗数量少，更显得弥足珍贵。

把诗写在琵琶背上，让人们联想到那著名的"烧槽琵琶"。李煜亲手把独一无二的烧槽琵琶放进了周后的棺中，与她合葬了。娥皇是个才情并茂的奇女子，让李煜念念一生而不能忘。传说她喝醉了酒即兴做琵琶曲，提笔一挥而就；又传说她善歌舞、工诗文、善制香。她年少时，正是因为一曲天籁般的琵琶演奏，让李煜的父亲赏爱无比，立刻将自己珍藏的烧槽琵琶送给了她，作为与六皇子李煜的定情物。婚后的整整十年里，李煜专宠娥皇一人。

Verse Written on Pipa Back Side

Your double shoulders are too narrow,
To arrange limited music strings in row.
Natural fragrance emits from your phoenix-tail,
Love warmth hidden in the wood box hole.

九月十日偶书[①]

晚雨秋阴酒乍醒，
感时心绪杳难平[②]。
黄花冷落不成艳，
红叶飕飕竞鼓声。
背世返能厌俗态，
偶缘犹未忘多情。
自从双鬓斑斑白，
不学安仁[③]却自惊。

【译注】

①此诗作于南唐行将灭亡之前，感时叶飘零，悲秋吐心声。李煜是虔诚的佛教徒，《九月十日偶书》中用过背世、俗态、偶缘（缘即因缘）等均为佛教用语。（选自《全唐诗》卷 8-5）

②杳（yǎo）难平：惆怅的样子。

③安仁：指西晋潘岳，字安仁，著名文学家，热衷于追求名利。（详见《晋书·潘岳传》）

Occasionally-Written Poem on September 10

The cloudy autumn awaken with a twilight
  rain,
Suddenly I feel uneasy with excitable emotion.
Not pretty but coldly withered is the chrysan-
  themum,
Red maple leaves sough as if lightly beating
  drum.
Without vulgar idea one could disgust vulgar
  state,
Never forget occasionally affectionate love
  fate.
Since my double sideburns turn into white,
I have not followed after Anren's* delight.

[Annotation]

*Anren was a famous writer in the West Jin Dynasty of China. His surname was Pan, first name Yue. (247 ~ 300)

病中感怀

憔悴年来甚，
萧条益自伤。
风威侵病骨，
雨气咽愁肠。
夜鼎唯煎药，
朝髭半染霜。
前缘竟何似，
谁与问空王①。

Lyric Verse of My Illness

I am haggard this year for my disease comes,
My mind depression has to do with self-injury.
The wind is so strong to penetrate my bones,
The gloomy rain swallows my hearty worry.
The tripod pot was used for boiling herbs at night,
The morning mustache was dyed with frost in white.
What a similarity, our fated suffering!
Who would like to ask the Buddha King?

【译注】

①空王：佛说世界一切皆空，尊称佛为“空王”。

病中书事[①]

病身坚固道情深，
宴坐清香思自任。
月照静居唯捣药[②]，
门扃[③]幽院只来禽。
庸医懒听词何取，
小婢将行力未禁。
赖问空门知气味，
不然烦恼万涂侵。

Memories of My Sickness

I sensed of deep love due to illness of my strong body,
Sitting to share delicious dinner to think of self- duty.
The moon shines over my silent house only for grinding herbs,
The door-closed secluded courtyard only flied over by birds.
A lazy doctor could not make a good diagnosis for his patient,
The young maid would try to care me but no medicinal talent.
Without learning from Buddhism to feel human's smell,
There would be no way to release too much self-sorrow.

【译注】

①此诗背景为抒发亡国之痛和故国之思。

②捣药：古代传说月亮上有白兔捣药。

③扃（jiōng）：（名）从外面关门的闩、钩等。

门扃：（动）扃门闭户，关门。

题金楼子后①

牙签万轴②裹红绡③，
王粲④书同付火烧。
不是祖龙留面目，
遗篇那得到今朝。

An Inscription to Gold-Pavilion Library

Myriad red silk works were full of ancient writing,
Wang Can's* books were destroyed by burning way.
If no book left to Emperor Qinshihuang, Yingzheng,
Then not any posthumous works would remain today.

【译注】

①这是李煜读罢《金楼子》写在书后的一首诗，此诗的主旨是对《金楼子》中提到的两件焚书事件发表感慨。

②牙签万轴：与汗牛充栋同义，形容书特多，所藏书籍繁富，不可胜数。

③绡：丝织物。[例句]风香绕路拂红绡，自拟长参寄具寮。

④王粲（177—217）：善诗文，其诗赋为建安七子之冠。《魏志》本传记王粲著诗、赋、论、议近60篇。有明人辑录遗文《王侍中集》。

[Annotation]

*Wang Can (177 to 217) was good at writing poetry or essay, and praised as an outstanding writer at that time.

渡中江望石城①泣下

江南江北旧家乡，
三十年来梦一场。
吴苑②宫闱今冷落，
广陵③台殿已荒凉。
云笼远岫④愁千片，
雨打归舟泪万行。
兄弟四人三百口，
不堪闲坐细思量。

Tearful Watching Stone City Ferry

Both of riversides are our old hometown,
Our imperial dream is thirty years long.
Kingdom Wu's palace being desolate today,
Guangling pavilions have been barren already.
Clouds shroud remote peaks with much sorrow,
Rain falls over the returned boat as if tears flow.
Four brothers with three-hundred people,
We must think hard but not to sit idle.

【译注】

①石城：南京。

②吴苑：宫阙名。

③广陵：今扬州。

④岫：峰峦。

残句（1）

迢迢牵牛星，
杳在河之阳。
粲粲黄姑女，
耿耿遥相望。
——见《癸辛杂识》

【译注】

首句分别为“迢迢牵牛星”“莺狂应有恨”（落花）“揖让月在手”（咏扇）“病态如衰弱”“衰颜一病难牵复”“万古到头归一死”“人生不满百”“日映仙云薄”“乌照始潜辉”“凝珠满露枝”等均隶属于所谓“句”或“残句”标题之下，其中只有第二、三“句”即“莺狂应有恨”“揖让月在手”有的版本加了《落花》《咏扇》标题。此英译本考虑到汉英对照排版的需要，人为地将诸“句”分隔开几部分。

Residual Poetic Lines (1)*

Far far away is the gloomy Altair Cowboy,
Standing at sunny side of the Milky Way.
Vega Weaving Girl glitters brightly,
Afar she is gazing at her love lovely.
—See<Micellaneous annotations
in Guixin Street>

[Annotation]

*Li Yu's "Residual Verses" from "Full Collection of Tang Poems" (Volume IIIV), which covered Southern Tang emperor Li Yu's verses (CI-poems as another kind of Chinese classical poetry) , and some residual verses were not exactly made sure as his own writing. In addition, some sentences or lines of poetry were collected from other classical books, such as "Guixin-Street Miscellaneous Annotations" and so on.

残句（2）落花

莺狂应有恨，
蝶舞已无多。
——题《落花》

Residual Poetic Lines (2)* Falling Flowers

Hatred must let the oriole crazily greedy,
Butterflies dancing freely are seldom angry.
—An inscription for <Falling Flowers>

[Annotation]

*The Song Dynasty poet Lu You wrote a book entitled Jottings of the everlasting learning academy, he pointed out that when Li Yu wrote the two lines of poetry pretty soon, the monarch's empire was tamed in subjugation.

残句（3）

咏扇

揖让月在手，
动摇风满怀。
——题《咏扇》

Residual Poetic Lines (3)*

Intoning a Paper Fan

Holding a fan as if the moon resting on hand,
To fan back and forth makes chest full of wind.
—An inscription of <Intoning a Paper Fan>

[Annotation]

*"Jottings on my secluded life in the stone forest" was written by the Song Dynasty author Ye Mengde. He said that the first Emperor of the Song Dynasty, Zhao Kuangyin praised Li Yu as a truly good member of imperial academy while Li Yu reciting his above-mentioned verse in the banquet.

残句（4）

病态如衰弱，
厌厌向五年。
——此句以下见《瀛奎律髓注》

Residual Poetic Lines (4)*

My ill expressions seem weak, not energetic,
It has lasted to the fifth year since being sick.
—See <Annotations on Tang-Song
Best Lyric Anthology>

[Annotation]

*The Yuan Dynasty writer Fang Hui compiled a book that covered the best poems of Tang and Song, and he made some annotation for the selected poetry.

残句（5）

衰颜一病难牵复，
晓殿君临颇自羞。
冷笑秦皇经远略，
静怜姬满苦时巡。
鬓从今日添新白，
菊是去年依旧黄。
——此句以下见《翰府名谈》

Residual Poetic Lines (5)

It is hard for a weak patient to recover better,
I am shy to enter the palace at daybreak later.
Coldly laughing Emperor Ying Zheng experienced farsighted strategy,
Silently sympathizing his empresses being bitter to seek for pity.
Nowadays my sideburns have a few hairs turn gray,
Chrysanthemum bloom as yellow as last year silently.
—See <Imperial Academy Famous Sayings>

残句（6）

万古到头归一死，
醉乡葬地有高原。
——有注云：煜岁暮乘醉书此于牖，醒而见之，大悔，不久谢世。

Residual Poetic Lines (6)

Even time goes on for 1000 years long,
Everyone will be heard of an elegy song.
To be buried in a highland,
His tipsy hometown.

残句（7）

人生不满百，
刚作千年画。
——见《野客丛谈》

Residual Poetic Lines (7)

Human longevity will be less than 100 years long,
The painted may have 1000 years to go down.
— See <Seclusion Literati Conversations>

残句（8）

日映仙云薄，
秋高天碧深。
——见《海录碎事》

Residual Poetic Lines (8)

The sunshine let fairy clouds thin over the heaven,
The autumn in the high sky looks deep and green.

—See <Widely-recorded unsystematic matters>

残句（9）

乌照始潜辉，
龙烛便争秉。
——此句以下见《孔帖》

Residual Poetic Lines (9)

The sun started emitting her hidden light,
The dragon-like candle was grasped tight.
— See <Confucian-compiled Anthology of Classic Works>

残句（10）

凝珠满露枝。
游飏日已西，
肃穆寒初至。
九重开扇鹄，
四牖炳灯鱼。
羽觞无算酌。
倾碗更为寿，
深卮递酬宾。

【译注】

以上诸“句”（“残句”）出处均见《全唐诗》卷八。

《老学庵笔记》《石林燕语》《瀛奎律髓注》，《翰府名谈》《野客丛谈》《海录碎事》《孔帖》等宋代著作中都能找到与李煜诗词有关的记载，对读者深入解读李煜作品颇有帮助。分别简介如下：

①《老学庵笔记》宋代陆游编著，十余卷，含“各家著录与论跋”并有明显褒贬朝政倾向。“只许州官放火，不许百姓点灯”的著名成语就是源于陆游借元宵节观灯之际讥讽州官留下

Residual Poetic Lines (10)

Sprigs full dews look to roll.
The sun flying to the western hill,
The serious climate is initially cold.
It is a nine-folding fan with a pictorial swan,
It is a four-window lantern like a fish pattern.
No drinking a cup of wine doesn’t mean an impolite discretion.
Trying to complete a bowl of wine means wish of longevity,
Filing wine into a deep cup expresses to reward guests friendly.

[Annotation]

(All the above poetry lines are selected from <Complete Collection of Tang Poetry>)

“Annotation in Old School Hut”, “Swallow-Speech in Stone Forest”, “Annotations on Tang-Song Best Lyric Anthology”, “Imperial Academy Famous Sayings”, “Seclusion Literati Conversations”, “Widely-recorded unsystematic matters”, “Confucian-compiled Anthology of Classic Works” and other works are to provide some index or hint of Emperor Li Yu poetry. To read the above-mentioned classical books, a careful reader can find some relevant records of Li Yu. Now here a few words used to introduce the seven ancient books as follows:

① "Annotation in Old School Hut" edited by Lu You in the Song Dynasty. The book consists of ten volumes, including "various bibliographic and postscript" and with a clear tendency to appraise the affairs of state. "Why, only allowed, not allowed to do anything,"(A magistrate allowed to burn down a citizen's house at night, but the house owner not allowed to light a lamp."只许州官放火，不许百姓点灯"）the famous saying is derived from poet Lu You's satire writings.

② "Swallow-Speech in Stone Forest" covers ten volumes written by Ye Mengde(1077~1148) in the Song Dynasty.

③ "Annotations on Tang-Song Best Lyric Anthology" is a general collection with Chinese five-character or seven-character poems selected and compiled by Fang Hui, in the Yuan Dynasty. (1227 ～ 1306)

④ "Imperial Academy Famous Sayings": The volume number was not known. The original book long lost. "Poetry-Chatting Summary" "Poets' Valuable Points" "Extensive Writings on Poetry Forest" and other ancient books used to copy some transcript of few poems from the book "Imperial Academy Famous Sayings" . So as for poetry, more good points were mentioned, such as "poetic sentences should not hinder the common truth" "the inside meaning is deep to help (used to praise an outstanding poet and high official Fan Zhongyan)" and

了"本州依例放火三日"妙笔而流行起来的。

②《石林燕语》：石林燕语十卷，宋叶梦得（1077-1148）撰。

③《瀛奎律髓注》：唐宋五七言律诗总集，元代方回(1227 ~ 1306)编选。

④《翰府名谈》不知卷数。原书久佚。《诗话总龟》《诗人玉屑》《诗林广记》等曾转录过该书中为数不多的诗词。该书论诗谓"佳句不应碍理"。称许范仲淹《赠钓者》诗，"实寓深意，不徒作也。"——据《中国历代诗话选》记载。

⑤《野客丛书》【宋】王茂撰三十卷，附《野老记闻一卷（浙江巡抚采进本）》，是考证典籍异同的书。

so on.

⑤ "Seclusion Literati Conversations" edited by Wang Mao, in the Song Dynasty. The book consists of thirty volumes and with an appendix as another volume entitled. "The Wild Elder's News Record". Wang Mao's book aimed at researching similarities and differences between more book.

⑥ "Widely-recorded unsystematic matters" contains twenty-two volumes compiled by the Song Dynasty scholar Ye Tinggui. The book is a medium-sized extraction of ancient series of books.

⑦ "Confucian-compiled Anthology of Classic Works " belonged to a large-sized comprehensive type of books. Actually, the book was just some parts of "Tang-and-Song dynasty combination works by Bai and Kong" (namely, poet Bai Juyi and Kong Chuan, one of Confucius' 42-generation grandson. Originally, Bai Juyi was the first to compile an anthology of classic writings and then Kong Chuan followed after Bai to do another similar anthology. Later, both anthologies combined into a united one, from which some of famous poems could be easily found in such a big book.

⑥《海录碎事》二十二卷，宋叶廷珪撰。《海录碎事》是一部中型类书，是宋代类书丛萃之一种。

⑦《孔帖》：隶属于南宋末年《唐宋白孔六帖》一部大型综合性类书。《白孔六帖》卷3“春”门《孔帖》是也。该书录有唐韦应物《长安遇冯著》等诗。

墓志铭①

呜呼！
庭兰伊何？
方春而零；
掌珠伊何②？
在玩而倾。
珠沉③媚泽，
兰陨芳馨。
人犹④沮恨，
我若为情。
萧萧极野，
寂寂重扃⑤。
与子长诀，
挥涕吞声。
噫嘻⑥哀哉！

Gravestone Epitaph

Alas!
How about you, my yard orchid?
Just now you spring flower withered.
A bright pearl in my palm,
Was soon fallen as a broken dream.
A pearl was going into a clear pool,
You orchid lost the fragrant smell.
The people were in sad regret,
My affectionate son was lost.
The wild field extremely desolate,
The door locked by a heavy bolt.
To my son, I say eternally farewell,
Let all my tears dry, not to flow.
Alas, eternally farewell.

【译注】

①李煜次子仲宣猝死于公元964年10月深秋，李煜亲自为爱子写了《墓志铭》。

②伊何：如何，为何，何人。

③沉：消失。

④犹：还。

⑤扃（jiōng）：从外面关门的闩、钩等。

⑥噫嘻：叹词。

亡后见形①诗

异国②非所志，
烦劳殊③清闲。
惊涛千万里，
无④乃见钟山。

The Subjugation Poem

Forced to move to a strange land is not my will,
Awaiting me is the trouble rather than going well.
Through myriad miles of surprising billows of ocean,
Zhongshan Mountain was eventually seen beyond my predictive imagination.

【译注】

①见形：现形；显露原形。

②异国：这里指自己覆灭的国家。

③殊：不同或超过。

④无：竟然。

昭惠周后诔①

天长地久，
嗟嗟蒸民②。

嗜欲既胜，
悲欢纠纷。

Eulogy to Queen Zhaohui Zhou

The heaven and globe last long and eternal,
Sighing deeply is the myriad common people.

They have presumptuous desire to be greedy,
Either joy or melancholy let them disharmony.

【译者按语 1】

李煜《昭惠周后诔》246 行，1313 个汉字，其中含 14 个重复出现的感叹词“呜呼哀哉”。总的行数多于白居易《长恨歌》两倍。

诔，即挽辞，哀挽死者的文体名，可兼容诗、文、曲、赋等形式。古代多用韵文。南唐后主所处的历史时期，据说人们惯于以诗的形式表述悲哀，虽然人们也不总是以词的形式表达欢快。实际上李煜扩大了词的功能，使词更富于表达不同感情色彩。

【译者按语 2】

为便于阅读时随时进行中英文对照，本书将长诗机械地分成若干小部分，这样也便于查找注释或译注。

缘情攸宅③，
触事来津④。

赀⑤盈世逸，
乐尠⑥愁殷。

The fated affectionate love is still what I yearn,
My lovesickness of you will permeate out again.

If wealth full, people felt comfortable and easy,
If joy less, they would be unhappy and melancholy.

【译注】

①诔（lěi）：挽诗或悼词。
②蒸民：众民，百姓。
③攸宅："攸"在此相当于"所"（所在）；"宅"含有依托、寄托之意。
④津：滋润、生发。
⑤赀（zī）：资财，财富。
⑥尠（xiǎn）：同"鲜"，稀有的，少见的。

[Annotation]

Li Yu' long poem, "Eulogy to Queen Zhaohui Zhou" has 246 lines, and 1,313 Chinese characters, including 14 recurring interjection "alas". The total number of poetry lines is two times greater than Bai Juyi long poem "Everlasting Regret".

The long poem was considered as a mourning speech or elegy, which was compatible with poetry, literature, music, and other forms of Fu-verse. In ancient times, such an elegy was usually written in rhyme. During South Tang historical period, the people are accustomed to express sorrow in the form of poetry, although it is not always expressed in the form of cheerful ci poetry. Emperor Li Yu expanded actual ci poetry of features that make the new poetry form more expressive in different emotions.

沉乌逞兔[7]，
茂夏凋春。

年弥念旷[8]，
得故忘新。

阙景[9]颓岸[10]，
世阅川奔。

外物交感，
犹伤昔人。

The setting sun looks up at the rising moon at night,
The spring is fading away, the lush summer day bright.

As long time goes on, the original love may be weaker,
However I still prefer the elder rather than the younger.

Eclipse happened, the mountain would be broken,
The world people would see the great flood run.

Everything eternal could be felt by man,
Even to hurt to ancient generations in pain.

【译注】

⑦沉乌逞兔：日落月升。

⑧年弥念旷：年久念淡。

⑨阙景：日食。

⑩颓岸：山崩。

诡梦高唐[11]，
诞夸洛浦[12]。

构[13]屈平虚，
亦悯终古。

况我心摧，
兴哀有地。

苍苍何辜，
歼予伉俪？

Gaotang city used to be dreamed wonderfully,
Luopu Goddess was praised absurdly boastfully.

Whether works factitious or true about the human,
Love sufferings would let the late generation in pain.

Moreover I seemed to be heartbroken,
Still my mind was full of a love ambition.

What sin motive let me go against the heaven?
Why God was to annihilate my favorite queen?

【译注】

⑪高唐：春秋时为齐国西境之一邑，迄今已有两千余年的历史。"诡梦高唐"是说高唐之梦诡异奇特（怀王巫山神女艳遇典）！

⑫诞夸洛浦：指传说中的洛浦女神未免有些浮夸或荒诞。

⑬构：泛指文艺作品。

窈窕难追，
不禄[14]于世。

玉泣珠融，
殒然破碎。

柔仪俊德，
孤映鲜双，

纤秾[15]挺秀，
婉娈[16]开阳[17]。

You were so gentle no one could be comparable,
You died so young that would be regrettable.

Pearls could be melting by jade warm tears.
Your died as if jewelry broken into pieces.

Your gentle manners with nice morality,
that could be unmatched in good quality.

Trees with tender blossoms tall and graceful,
My queen seemed to be brightly beautiful.

【译注】

⑭不禄——天子死曰崩，诸侯死曰薨，大夫死曰卒，士(死)曰不禄。——《礼记·曲礼》

⑮纤秾：花木细嫩茂密。

⑯婉娈(wǎn luán)：亦作婉恋，美貌。

⑰开阳：前面没有遮挡阳光的物体。能有日光照耀的地方。

艳不至冶[18]，
慧或无伤。

盘绅[19]奚[20]戒，
慎肃惟常。

环佩[21]爱节，
造次[22]有章。

会颦发笑，
擢秀腾芳。

Being so gorgeous, but not flirtatious,
Full of wisdom, but not treacherous.

A long-fluttering belt was going around your jade-body,
The dignified solemn attire reflected your daily beauty.

The jingle jade pendant was heard of the rhythmic,
Speedy melody sounded into the harmony music.

Knitting your brows formed a sweet smile, your charming more attractive than any girl.
Being so gorgeous, but not flirtatious, full of wisdom, but not treacherous.

【译注】

⑱冶：形容女子装饰艳丽（含贬义）—冶艳、妖冶。

⑲绅：古代束在腰间的大带子。

⑳奚：如何，怎么，什么，为什么。

㉑环佩：通常指玉饰或美女。

㉒造次：匆忙、仓促。

鬓云留鉴，
眼彩飞光。

情漾春媚，
爱语风香。

瑰姿禀异，
金冶昭祥。

婉容无犯，
均教多方。

The cloud-like sideburns were hidden in mirror,
Your double lively eyes still so brightly glitter.

An affectionate beauty would flirt the bright spring,
Your lyric chat was as sweet as vernal breeze blowing.

The pretty gesture reflected your unique character,
As if gold was tempered to become much brighter.

The graceful appearance had no flaw at all,
That could teach more people to behave well.

茫茫独逝，
舍我何乡？

In the vast universe, alone you passed away,
Where could I go when you left me lonely?

昔我新婚，
燕尔[23]情好。

Initially when our newlywed started,
Our affectionate love were so perfect.

媒无劳辞，
筮[24]无违报。

No need, matchmaker talked much repeatedly,
The fortuneteller had nothing unlucky to say.

归妹[25]邀终，
咸[26]爻[27]协兆。

Guimei-Trigram foretold our newlywed to be eternal,
Xian-Trigram showed the fated harmonious symbol.

【译注】

㉓燕尔：欢乐的样子。

㉔筮（shì）：古代用蓍草占卜为筮法。

㉕归妹：《易经》类著述中提到的杂卦名——归妹——"女之终也"。

㉖咸：咸、恒为第三十一与第三十二卦。《杂卦传》云："咸，速也；恒，久也。"（《归妹》卦说我们会白头到老，《咸》卦也表达了相同的意思）

㉗爻（yáo）：组成八卦的长短横道。

俯仰同心， 绸缪是道。	Two minds think alike in the same way, Lingering affectionately in a love way.
执子之手， 与子偕老。	Your hands I hold, Until we grow old.
今也如何， 不终往告？ 呜呼哀哉，	Nowadays，how about you? The happy prediction turned zero. Alas, sorrow!
志心既违， 孝爱克全。	Our everlasting wish could not come true, Love and filial piety hardly carried through.

殷勤柔握[28]，
力折危言。

遗情眄眄，
哀泪涟涟。

何为忍心，
览此哀编。

绝艳易凋，
连城易脆。

You are so gentle and so affectionate,
To strongly beat slandered statement.

Your last love kept on lingering affectionately,
Drop by drop, you shed endless tears quietly.

Why you so hard-hearted to leave me lonely?
Did you silently read my heartbroken eulogy?

Beautiful flowers would be easily to fade away,
Priceless brittle jewelry would be broken easily.

【译注】

㉘柔握：柔美的手。指代女子。晋陶潜［例句］忆盈盈倩笑，纤纤柔握，玉香花语，雪暖酥凝。

实曰能容， 壮心是醉。	You had been magnanimous and tolerant, You intoxicated me as an ambitious talent.
信美堪餐， 朝饥[29]是慰。	So beautiful as delicious food to lure me to eat, You let me comfortably meet my hungry belly.
如何一旦， 同心旷世？ 呜呼哀哉！	How could I imagine just within a day, my affectionate love passed away? Alas, so unhappy!
丰才富艺， 女也克肖[30]。	Rich in art talent and creative quality, Vividly you cloned a versatile beauty.

【译注】

㉙朝饥：早晨空腹时感到的饥饿。

㉚克肖：相似。

采戏[31]传能， 弈棋逞妙。	Your lottery-play seemed magic, Chess game's also quite unique.
媚动占相， 歌萦柔调。	Your dancing posture was lively graceful, Your mellowed voice heard to be beautiful.
兹鼗[32]爰质， 奇器传华。	The Qiuci-drum's well-known for its lovely quality, Such a unique instrument spread in China widely.
翠虬[33]一举， 红袖飞花。	When you dance in graceful gestures vividly, Your red sleeves like flowers to bloom freely.

【译注】

㉛采戏：掷骰赌采为戏。（娥皇擅长琵琶、采戏、弈棋等，无不妙绝。）

㉜兹鼗（cí táo）：汉代西域国龟兹（qiū cí）出的一种鼓。古龟兹在今新疆库车一带。

㉝翠虬：这里指娥皇的舞姿。

情驰天际，
思栖云涯。

发扬掩抑，
纤紧洪奢。

穷幽极致，
莫得微瑕。

审音者仰止，
达乐者兴嗟。

Your affectionate love was gone to paradise,
Our lovesickness settled along cloudy skyline.

With charming rhythm，it’s your pleasant song,
The extravagant tone, now gentle and then strong.

Your elegant shows were with endless charm,
That could not be pointed any flaws of them.

The music reviewer gazed admiringly,
The wise observer praised you highly.

曲演来迟，
破[34]传邀舞，

利拨[35]迅手，
吟商[36]呈羽[37]。

制革常调，
法移往度。

翦遏繁态，
蔼成新矩。

You were late to sing a song as a show,
I wondered being invited to dance with you.

Your deft hand played chess fast,
You rewrote dancing lyrics best.

Making evolution renewed the routine classic melody,
Adjusting the old dance tune by a new methodology.

Simplifying some complicated artistic creation,
could turn into new works through revision.

【译注】

㉞破：突破（规定、习惯、思想等）；破例。

㉟拨：指下棋出子。

㊱商：古代五音之一，这里用来指代曲谱。

㊲羽：指代娥皇整理修补失传的《霓裳羽衣舞》曲。

霓裳旧曲，
韬音沦世，

失味齐音，
犹伤孔氏。

故国遗声，
忍乎湮坠。

我稽㊳其美，
尔扬其秘。

Colourful Plumage* used to be an ancient song,
As a dancing song, it was not handed down.

The lost tune was once with hereditary perfect music,
That's not inferior to Confucious period's rhythmic lyric.

The hereditary song was handed down in the Tang,
Such a native song should not be tolerable to drown.

I try to research on its valuable beauty,
You do best to expose its inner secret.

【译注】

㊳稽：考核，考查。

[Annotation]

*Colourful Plumage is an ancient dancing song popular in the palace of the Tang Dynasty, which was written by Emperor Li Longji...His famous concubine Yang Yuhuan was good at singing and dancing. The song used to accompany her to dance.

程度馀律，	Restoring the classic rhythmic melody,
重新雅制。	Renewed the music in elegant quality.
非子而谁，	Only you and I characterised by similarity,
诚吾有类。	Only both of us had the same hobby.
今也则亡，	Nowadays you have gone far far away,
永从遐逝。	You will have no home-going day.
呜呼哀哉！	Alas, no back way.

该兹[39]硕美， 郁[40]此芳风，	You have turned into a graceful mellowed beauty, As if fragrant lush blossoms blooming with the windy.
事传遐禩[41]， 人难与同。	Worshipping of you will be eternal, No one's quality can match with you.
式瞻[42]虚馆[43]， 空寻所踪。	Enviously to watch the empty palace, It' s impossible to find your lively trace.
追悼良时， 心存目忆。	I mourned to recall for a while, My mind and heart full of you.
景旭雕薨[44]， 风和绣额。	The morning sunshine is shrouding over your dead body, The breeze combs your embroidery-like sideburns silently.

【译注】

㊴兹：这个，现在。

㊵郁：香气浓厚；（草木）茂盛。

㊶遐禩 (xiá sì)：长久祭祀（禩同祀）。

㊷式瞻：敬仰，景慕。

㊸虚馆：寂静的馆舍。此处指代寝宫。

㊹薨（hōng）：古代称诸侯之死为薨，后世被封爵的大官之死也称薨。

燕燕[45]交音，
洋洋[46]接色。

A couple of swallows are singing harmoniously,
Both of them look at each other affectionately.

蝶乱落花，
雨晴寒食。

Butterflies are dancing until flowers falling,
Cold Food Festival is coming after raining.

接辇[47]穷欢，
是宴是息。

We pushed a cart back and forth to be pleasant,
We used to share a feast or enjoy a good rest.

含桃[48]荐实，
畏日流空。

The cherries became ripe in red dye,
The scorching sun shining in the sky.

【译注】

㊺燕燕：《诗经》有“燕燕于飞”句。

㊻洋洋：形容众多或丰盛。

㊼辇（niǎn）：古人拉或推的车。

㊽含桃：樱桃的别称。

林雕晚箨[49]，
莲舞疏红。

烟轻丽服，
雪莹修容。

纤眉范月，
高髻凌风。

辑柔尔颜，
何乐靡从[50]？

Flowery pattern carved on bamboos' skin,
The dancing lotuses' red color was thin.

Cloud-like gentle dress reflected your beauty,
Graceful appearance's like snow-like jewelry.

Your slender brows simulating the crescent,
Your bun by wind blowing reached top height.

You had such a gentle and agreeable look,
That nowhere would be possible to seek.

【译注】

㊾箨 (tuò)：竹笋的外层或竹皮。

㊿靡从（mí cóng）：无从，没有门径或头绪。

蝉响吟愁，
槐凋落怨。

四气(51)穷哀，
萃此秋宴。

我心无忧，
物莫能乱。

弦乐清商(52)，
艳尔醉盼。

The noisy sad cicadas sang time and again,
The withered leafs lost resentments hidden.

One's emotion may be sad as four seasons alter,
However, flowery plants share the autumn dinner.

Not any trouble occupied my mind,
Everything goes well in good order.

You play with Pipa to the Pure Palace Melody,
As crazy as you seemed to be a tipsy beauty.

【译注】

(51)四气：又称四性，指寒热温凉影响人体阴阳盛衰。

(52)清商：清乐，也称为清商乐，是指汉魏六朝的乐府音乐，流传下来的歌词即当时的乐府诗。

情如何其，
式(53)歌且宴。

寒生蕙(54)幄，
雪舞兰堂。

珠笼(55)暮卷，
金炉夕香。

丽尔渥丹(56)，
婉尔清扬(57)。

Then we were how happy and cheerful,
Singing and sharing a delicious meal.

Growing in cold tent is the fragrant cymbidium,
Dancing like snowing is the orchid in bloom.

The cage pearl curtain was rolled down at dusk,
At sunset in censer, we burnt the incense stick.

Your rosy cheeks look beautiful,
Your eyes bright with brows gentle.

【译注】

(53)式：典礼，有特定内容的仪式。

(54)蕙，即蕙兰，一种香草蕙兰。幄(wò)：帐幕。

(55)珠笼：缀珠而成的鸟笼。

(56)渥丹：润泽光艳的朱砂，多形容红润的面色。

(57)清扬：眉清目朗。

厌厌[58]夜饮，
予何尔忘？

年去年来，
殊欢逸赏[59]。

如何倏然[60]，
已为畴曩[61]？
呜呼哀哉！

At a bustling night we drank a lot,
How could both of us forget it?

Year in and year out,
We indulge in fun a lot.

How time flies without a moment slow,
Everything seemed to happen few days ago.
Alas, with my sorrow!

【译注】

㊺厌厌：整齐茂盛貌；秀美貌。

㊻殊欢逸赏：纵情玩乐。

㊼倏然（shū·rán）：极快、倏忽、须臾、忽然、瞬间。

㊽畴曩（chóu nǎng）：往日；旧时。

孰谓逝者， 荏苒弥疏。	Don't say if a person passed away, Soon the dead would be faded away.
我思姝子[62]， 永念犹初。	I would miss you, an eternal love beauty, I would ever hide your initial good memory.
寒暑斯疚， 吾宁御诸[63]？ 呜呼哀哉！	Still lovesick no matter how seasons changeable, I would advise high officials as calm as possible. Alas, possible!

【译注】

㉜姝子：美女。

㉝御诸：指与皇帝或宫廷有关的人或事。

万物无心， 风烟若故。	Everything willful is heartless, Self-willed wind is shapeless.
惟日惟月， 以阴以雨。	Only the sun and the moon seen in the dome, Rain or shine, not to change their own form.
事则依然， 人乎何所？	Everything will remain to happen, Where will I seek for my queen?
悄悄房栊， 孰堪其处？ 呜呼哀哉！	Your palace living room remained as before in silence, Who would like to be calm in such a place? Alas!

佳名镇在， 望月伤娥。	Your beautiful name will be eternal, Looking up at the moon sadly, I miss you.
双眸永隔， 见镜无波。	Your double eyes would be no longer open, The mirror had no your leering at me again.
皇皇[64]望绝， 心如之何？	Disappointed for your fashionable style lost, Who knows what I would like to think about?
暮树苍苍， 哀摧[65]无际。	Under the vast twilight, trees look gray and hazy, My mind is full of endless sadness and melancholy.
历历前欢， 多多遗致[66]，	The past joy turned into good memory, As if myriad shows left in eyes vividly.

【译注】

⑭皇皇：同〔惶惶〕遑遑。形容堂皇；盛大。

⑮哀摧：哀伤；悲痛。

⑯多多遗致：历历在目。

丝竹声悄，
绮罗[67]香杳[68]。

想淡乎忉怛[69]，
恍越乎悴憔。
呜呼哀哉！

The Pipa melody sound vanishing quietly,
The silk garments' fragrance faded away.

In order to relieve my great pain silently,
I had to sink into a haggard state calmly.
Alas, sadly!

【译注】

⑥⑦绮罗（qǐ luó）：丝织物。[例句]生小调丝竹，由来足绮罗。

⑥⑧杳（yǎo）：（形）昏暗；远得不见踪影。

⑥⑨忉怛（dāo dá）：忧伤，悲痛。

岁云暮兮，
无相见期。

情瞀[70]乱兮，
谁将因依！

维[71]昔之时兮亦如此，
维今之心兮不如斯[72]。
呜呼哀哉！

The year clouds will fly till twilight,
We will have no chance to reunite.

My affectionate heart sunk in disorder,
Who would understand and take care?

In the past days, I used to be happy to meet you,
Nowadays my mind's full of a terrible sorrow.
Alas, a terrible sorrow!

【译注】

⑦瞀（mào）：看不清楚，心情混乱。

㉑维：〈助〉用于句首，表示意念的衔接、维系。

㉒如斯：如此。

神之不仁兮，
敛怨为德。

既取我子兮，
又毁我室。

镜重轮兮何年，
兰袭香兮何日？
呜呼哀哉！

Heartless god is not benevolent in its quality,
Resentments to decrease may be as its morality.

God captured not only my young son,
But also destroyed my favorite queen.

Which year the broken mirror restored again?
Which day the withered orchid fragrant as often?
Alas, my queen!

天漫漫兮愁云曀，
空暧暧兮愁烟起。

娥眉[73]寂寞兮闭佳城，
哀寝悲气兮竟徒尔。
呜呼哀哉！

日月有时兮，
龟蓍[74]既许，

箫笳凄咽兮，
旗常是举。

龙輀[75]一驾兮无来辕，
金屋千秋兮永无主。
呜呼哀哉！

In the vast heaven, gloomy clouds cease to flow,
In the warm sky, thin mists rise up with sorrow.

My beautiful queen felt lonely to close the tomb,
Her sighing was in vain within the coffin room.
Alas, in gloom!

The sun and the moon move, as time going on,
The divination had foretold our marriage long.

In a sad and choked melody, Shaw-Jia at playing,
The white banner of mourning held up in fluttering.

Your funeral cart will never go back again,
No one will long live in your gold-like coffin.
Alas, in pain!

【译注】

⑬娥眉（é méi）：也作蛾眉。旧指美人。
⑭龟蓍（guī shī）：龟甲和蓍草。古代占卜之具。
⑮龙輀（lóng ér）：帝王的丧车。

木交枸兮风索索，
鸟相鸣兮飞翼翼。

吊孤影兮孰我哀，
自怜兮痛无极。
呜呼哀哉！

A pair of wolfberries were born twin to the wind blowing,
A pair of lovebirds, wing to wing, were flying and singing.

Oh, no one is sadder than I mourn your lonely shadow,
Oh, I am endlessly lovesick at you in too much sorrow.
Alas, too much sorrow.

夜寤皆感兮， 何响不哀？	Sleepless all over the night,still I miss you, Everything I heard was nothing but sorrow.
穷求弗[76]获兮， 此心隳摧[77]。	I tried to seek for you, but nothing to win, I was heartbroken of my love affection.
号无声兮何续， 神永逝兮长乖[78]。 呜呼哀哉！	What else could I do besides sobbing silently? My sweetheart goddess eternally passed away. Alas, sadly!

【译注】

⑯弗：不。

⑰隳摧（huī cuī）：犹坍塌。“殿宇半隳摧，门临野水开”。

⑱长乖：永别。多指死亡，与世长乖。

杳杳[79]香魂，
茫茫天步[80]，

抆血[81]抚榇[82]，
邈子何所？

苟云路之可穷，
冀[83]传情于方士[84]！
呜呼哀哉！

Your scented soul will rest in the eternal deep calm,
Your skyline step will reach the heavenly vast dome.

Through bloodletting I touch and feel your coffin,
Where I will be to seek for you, my favorite queen?

If the fairy road were to reach the heaven,
Daoists would bring my love to you again.
Alas, with my pain!

【译注】

⑲杳杳 (yǎo yǎo)：深远幽暗。“苍苍竹林寺，杳杳钟声晚”。

⑳天步：天之行步。泛指时运（一时的运气）。朱熹集传：“步，行也。天步，犹言时运也。”

㉑抆血 (wěn xuè)：擦拭血泪。常用于讣闻，表示极其哀痛。抆血较拭泪为重。

㉒榇 (chèn)：棺材。

㉓冀：希望，希冀。

㉔方士：亦称术士，后来称道士。古时被认为是可以升天入地、善于沟通天上人间的神通广大之士。

第二部分　词

Part Two Ci Poems

渔父
（浪花有意千重雪）

浪花有意千重雪，
桃李无言一队春。
一壶酒，一竿纶，
世上如侬有几人？

Old Fisherman

White waves want to be the 1000-flake snow,
Silent peaches and plums stand in a spring row.
Drinking a pot of wine, holding a fishing-rod hook,
In the world, few men do so, whom did I ask?

【译注】

渔父：渔翁，捕鱼的老人。渔父等字样最早出现在《史记·屈原贾生列传》。

此词以渔夫的清高绝傲反衬诗人在心灵上是自由的、孤傲的。只要有一壶酒、一叶舟、一帆春风、一竿轻丝、一弯钩，就能够拥有全部的自己。这恰是帝王所向往的。

渔父[1]
（一棹春风一叶舟）

一棹[2]春风一叶舟，
一纶[3]茧缕[4]一轻钩。
花满渚[5]，酒满瓯[6]，
万顷波中得自由。

【译注】

①此词调名亦作《渔父词》《渔歌子》。

②棹（zhào）：摇船的工具。短的叫楫，长的叫棹。

③纶：钓鱼用的粗丝线。

④茧缕（lǚ）：丝线，这里指渔弦。

⑤渚（zhǔ）：水中间的小块陆地。

⑥瓯（ōu）：酒盅，一种平底深碗。

Old Fisherman

A gust of spring breeze paddles a leaf-like boat,
A long thick fishing line links a hook in float.
The isle is fully flowery, the wine cups filled fully,
Ten-thousand-acres waves unrestrained freely.

浣溪沙①
（红日已高三丈透）

红日已高三丈透，
金炉次第添香兽②。
红锦地衣随步皱。

佳人舞点金钗溜。
酒恶时③拈花蕊嗅。
别殿遥闻箫鼓奏。

Washing-Creek-Sand

Rising up thirty-foot high is the red sun,
Incenses inserted in the censer to burn.
Dancers' paces made red brocade carpet
wrinkle.

The hair-pin, loosen, lost, dancing girls didn't
know.
They were so tipsy to smell the blooming
pistil.
The flute and drum were heard in another hall.

【译注】

①浣溪沙，唐教坊曲名，因春秋时期美女西施浣纱于若耶溪而得名，亦作"浣溪纱""小庭花"等。（若耶溪源于浙江若耶山，北流入运河。相传为西施浣纱之所。）

②香兽：向兽形香炉里添香。

③酒恶时：酒喝多了。

木兰花[1]

（晚妆初了明肌雪）

晚妆初了明肌雪[2]，
春殿嫔娥鱼贯列。
笙箫吹断水云闲，
重按霓裳歌遍彻。

临春谁更飘香屑，
醉拍阑干情味切。
归时休放烛花红，
待踏马蹄清夜月。

【译注】

①《木兰花》：与《玉楼春》《春晓曲》《惜春容》为同调。

②明肌雪：形容肌肤明洁细腻，洁白如雪。

Spring in Jade Pavilion

(another title <Magnolia>)

Makeup was done, snowy white cheeks of concubines,
The spring palace imperial beauties formed a long line.
The phoenix flute in play made idle misty clouds to fly,
Colorful Plumage Song sung loud thoroughly in the sky.

Against the wind, who would emit more fragrant smell?
He seemed to be tipsy, senselessly to pat the railing-handle.
Back home, he would not be busy to burn a candle,
But to ride a horse to touch the night moon to go.

一斛①珠
（晚妆初过）

晚妆初过，
沈檀[2]轻注些儿个。
向人微露丁香颗[3]，
一曲清歌，
暂引樱桃破[4]。

One Gok of Beads

Her morning makeup just done,
Lips lightly painted by a lipstick of crimson.
She stuck out fragrant clove-violet tongue,
Singing in her clear tone,
Her cherry-like small mouth open.

【译注】
（首行"晚妆"：亦有"晓妆"版本。）
①斛（hú）：自秦汉一斛为十斗，南宋末年一斛改为五斗。斛和石相通。
②沈檀：绛色的唇膏。
③丁香颗：指美女舌头。
④樱桃破：张开樱桃小口。

罗袖裛[⑤]残殷色可，
杯深旋被香醪涴[⑥]。
绣床斜凭娇无那[⑦]，
烂嚼红茸[⑧]，
笑向檀郎[⑨]唾。

Wine drops wetted her silk sleeves in black,
Soon another big cup of wine she drank.
Leaning upon her embroidery bed in her gentle charming manner,
Dangling a red hair-band,
Smiling at her dear lover.

【译注】

⑤裛（yì）：古同“浥”。沾湿；缠裹；用香熏。［例句］麝裛战袍香。

⑥醪（láo）：浊酒。涴（wò）：弄脏。

⑦无那：无奈。

⑧红茸：红色的丝线。

⑨檀郎：古代妇女称其所爱男子为檀郎。

采桑子
（亭前春逐红英尽）

亭前春逐红英尽，
舞态徘徊。
细雨霏微，
不放双眉时暂开。

绿窗冷静芳音断，
香印成灰。
可奈情怀，
欲睡朦胧入梦来。

Picking Mulberries

In front of the palace pavilion, spring breeze blows red flowers fallen,
A dancing girl wanders time and again.
Lingering on is the rain,
Her frown double brows open.

Yet no sweet voice heard, near the window in green,
Her incense sticks burnt, leaving ashes as often.
She could not help being lovesick,
Her drowsy hazy dream romantic.

【译注】

该词写少妇伤春怀人、愁思难遣情怀，以妇人之恨见妇人之心，以妇人之心见妇人之愁，情景相映，意境哀婉深沉。

清平乐
（别来春半）

别来春半，
触目柔肠断。
砌下[①]落梅如雪乱，
拂了一身还满。

雁来音信无凭，
路遥归梦难成。
离恨恰如春草，
更行更远还生。

【译注】

①砌下：阶下。

Purely Monotonous Music

Half a spring has gone away since our separation,
Reunion would let two hearts broken again.
Plum blossoms fell on stone steps in random,
The whole body fully covered by the blossom.

I wondered if the wild geese would send a letter,
My back home dream was a long road to wander.
The parting regret seemed to be fresh grass vernal.
The more to spread over, the more they would grow.

喜迁莺
（晓月坠）

晓月坠，
宿云微，
无语枕边攲[1]。
梦回芳草思依依，
天远雁声稀。

啼莺散，
余花乱，
寂寞画堂深院。
片红休扫尽从伊，
留待舞人归。

Love-Migrating Orioles

The morning moon just fallen,
The night clouds thin,
Upon my pillow, I silently lean.
Dreaming of fragrant grass,
my mind was full of lovesickness,
The sky afar was with rare sounds of wild geese.

Singing orioles were flying to scatter,
Residual flowers fell in disorder,
The deep courtyard was with a gallery.
Red falling petals not cleaned away,
In order to let a dancer pleasantly.

【译注】

①攲（qī）：倾斜。

菩萨蛮①
（花明月暗笼轻雾）

花明月暗笼轻雾，
今宵好向郎边去。
刬袜[2]步香阶，
手提金缕鞋。

画堂南畔见，
一向偎人颤。
奴为出来难，
教君恣意怜。

Beautiful and Long-Haired Dancers

Under the misty dome, flowers look bright,
the moon dim,
Tonight she went upstairs.
She did not put on gold-thread shoes,
Only on her socks to enter the bedroom.

Meeting at the gallery hall south,
Both of them emotionally embrace.
As a maid, I am not easy to see you,
I beg monarch to pity my shy sorrow.

【译注】

①“菩萨蛮”词牌源于唐宣宗（李忱）年间，女蛮国派遣使者进贡，她们身上披挂着珠宝，头上戴着金冠，梳着高高的发髻，号称“菩萨蛮队”，当时教坊就因此制成《菩萨蛮曲》，后来《菩萨蛮》就成了词牌名。亦作《菩萨鬘》，原指舞女头发又美又长。

此词李煜创作于公元964年（北宋乾德二年）前后，描写与小周后幽会的情景。

②刬(chǎn)袜：以袜贴地。刬同“铲”。不穿鞋子，踩着袜子走路叫刬袜。

菩萨蛮
（蓬莱院闭天台女）

蓬莱院闭天台女①，
画堂②昼寝人无语。
抛枕③翠云④光，
绣衣闻异香。

潜来珠锁⑤动，
惊觉银屏梦⑥。
脸慢⑦笑盈盈，
相看无限情。

Beautiful and Long-Haired Dancers

In the Penglai Fairy Palace locked a fairy maiden,
Within the gallery at daytime slept a young man.
Cloud-like hairs' light over her thrown-off pillow,
Her embroidery dresses were to emit unique smell.

The man came secretly to click the pearl knocker,
The romantic maiden dream's broken by stranger.
Her pretty face flushed in smiling,
They wink at each other in love feeling.

【译注】

①蓬莱：古代传说中的仙山。天台女：指仙女，像仙女一样美丽的女子。

②画堂：汉代宫中的殿堂，后用以泛指绘饰华丽的堂屋。

③抛枕：熟睡时头离开了枕头，把它抛在一边。

④翠云：女子的头发。宋代柳永《洞仙歌》中有句："记得翠云偷剪，和鸣彩凤于飞。"云：云髻。

⑤潜来：偷偷地进来，暗中来。珠锁：用珍珠连缀而成或有珍珠镶饰的门环。

⑥银屏梦：这里指好梦。

⑦脸慢：指细嫩而美丽的脸。慢同"曼"，形容容颜的美好。

菩萨蛮
（铜簧韵脆锵寒竹）

铜簧韵脆锵寒竹①，
新声②慢奏移纤玉③。
眼色暗相钩④，
秋波⑤横欲流。

【译注】

①铜簧：乐器中发声的铜片。锵：乐器的音响。寒竹：指乐器。

②新声：此处犹指李煜大周后娥皇整理出的《霓裳羽衣曲》。

③纤玉：比喻美女纤细洁白如玉的手指。

④钩：同“勾”，招引。

⑤秋波：别作“娇波”，如秋水半清澈的目光。

Beautiful and Long-Haired Dancers

The copper reed’s crisp rhyme with the cold
bamboo flute melody,
New song slowly strummed by gentle fingers
of the beautiful lady.
Tacit agreement by eyes’ secret wink,
With a sidelong lecherous look.

雨云[⑥]深绣户，
未便谐衷素[⑦]。
宴罢[⑧]又成空，
梦迷[⑨]春雨中。

Clouds lust for rain in a pretty mansion,
Where it is not convenient to make a lovely fun.
After pleasure, flirting turned nothing.
Lecherous dream vanished in rainy spring.

【译注】

⑥雨云：降雨的云，此处暗指男女情爱。

⑦未便：未即，没有立即。别作“来便”。谐：谐和。衷素：内心的真情。衷：内心。素：通“愫”，真情。

⑧宴罢：欢乐之后。

⑨梦迷：别作“魂迷”。春雨：别作“春睡”“春梦”。

子夜歌①
（寻春须是先春早）

寻春须是先②春早，
看花莫待花枝老。
缥色③玉柔④擎，
醅⑤浮盏面清⑥。

Midnight Song

It is necessary to seek for spring ahead of her arrival,
To look at her scenery, do not wait for all flowers fall.
The Sapphire Blue wine glass held up by gentle fingers,
The unstrained wine filled in the cup with surface clear.

【译注】

①此词调名《历代诗余》中作《菩萨蛮》(子夜歌)。
②先：要寻春就应该在春天到来之前。
③缥色：青白色（酒）。
④玉柔：女人洁白柔嫩的手。
⑤醅（pēi）：没有过滤的酒，这里泛指酒。
⑥清：旧抄本中“清”的占位为一空格。吕远本、萧江声抄本分别在《南唐二主词》《历代诗余》两书中加补了“清”字。

何妨频笑粲⑦，
禁苑⑧春归晚。
同醉与闲评⑨，
诗随羯鼓⑩成。

Why we'll not heartily laugh?
The forbidden garden's spring will slowly leave.
Let us share being tipsy and chat freely,
Let us beat Jie drum and recite poetry.

【译注】

⑦粲（càn）：频频地欢笑。粲，笑貌，露齿而笑或大笑。

⑧禁苑：封建帝王的园林。

⑨闲评：随意品评、议论，即没有固定题目的自由评论。

⑩羯（jié）鼓：亦作叠鼓或揭鼓，是唐代很盛行的一种打击乐器，起源于印度。《通典·乐四》中有记载："羯鼓，正如漆桶，两头俱击。"羯，是中国古代少数民族之一，曾附属匈奴，此鼓因出于羯，所以称之为羯鼓。

采桑子

（辘轳金井梧桐晚）

辘轳金井梧桐晚，
几树惊秋，
昼雨新愁，
百尺虾须①在玉钩。

琼窗春断双蛾皱，
回首边头，
欲寄鳞游②，
九曲寒波不溯流。

Picking Mulberries

Late phoenix parasol locates at the windlass well,
Few trees wonder the autumn arrival.
The daytime drizzle lures me new sorrow.
The curtain jade hooks link the lobster-like tail.

The jade window with spring views broken, her double brows frown, not so open,
Looking back the remote region,
Let swimming fish send my letter by the zigzag running water.

【译注】

①“虾须，帘也。”唐代陆畅《帘》诗中有例句“劳将素手卷虾须，琼室流光更缀珠”。
②鳞游：游鱼，指代书信。古人有“鱼传尺素”之说。

谢新恩
（金窗力困起还慵）
（一）

□□□□□□□□，
□□□□□□□。
□□□□□□□□。

□□□□，
□□□□□□。

□□□□□□□□，
金窗[1]力困起还慵[2]。
□□□□，
□□□□□□。

Thanks for New Bestowing (1)

□□□□□□□□,
□□□□□□□.
□□□□□□□□.

□□□□,
□□□□□□.

□□□□□□□□,
Still sleepy, lazy to get up though windows bright.
□□□□,
□□□□□□.

【译注】

①金窗：亦作“金牕”，华美的窗。

②慵：同“慵”。困倦，懒。

【译注】

不同版本普遍录有六首《谢新恩》，其一只有“金窗力困起还慵”一行，而这一行的内容与第三首中的一行完全一样，如此 似乎可以认为其一与其三是同一首。

谢新恩
（秦楼不见吹箫女）
（二）

秦楼不见吹箫女①，
空余上苑②风光。
粉英金蕊自③低昂④。
东风恼我，
才发一襟⑤香。

Thanks for New Bestowing (2)

The Phoenix Watchtower without a girl playing flute,
The empty Upper Garden scenery is desolate.
Lowering heads, flowers bloomed in white, pistils in yellow,
The maiden lovesick by a gust of east wind with fragrance in blow.

琼窗□[6]梦留残日，
当年得恨何长！
碧阑干外映垂杨。
暂时相见，
如梦懒[7]思量。

The jade window seemed to block her dream
broken, leaving a residual sun.
Then she hated it shone too long in the heaven,
The poplars' shadow lay upon the railing in
green.
Reuniting was just a bit of luck,
I dreamed of being lazy to think.

【原注】

王国维辑本《南唐二主词》校勘记：此首实系《临江仙》调。

【译注】

①秦楼：秦穆公为其女弄玉所建之楼，亦称凤凰台。吹箫女：即弄玉，古有弄玉吹箫乘凤而去的典故，故后人以此来表示人去楼空，睹物思人之情。

②上苑：帝王园林。

③粉英：别版误作“粉莫”。粉英金蕊，指各种颜色的花。自：各自。

④低昂：高低起伏。

⑤襟：衣领。

⑥缺字不可考。

⑦懒：别版误作“嫩”“娥”。

谢新恩
（庭空客散人归后）
（三）

庭空客散人归后，
画堂半掩珠帘。
林风淅淅夜厌厌[①]。
小楼新月，
回首自纤纤[②]。

春光镇[③]在人空老，
新愁往恨何穷？
金窗[④]力困起还慵[⑤]。
一声羌笛，
惊起醉怡容。

【原注】

王国维辑本《南唐二主词》校勘记：此亦《临江仙》调。（此首“春光”以下应作另一首。）

【译注】

①厌厌：整齐茂盛；秀美。

②纤：细小，细微。

④金窗：亦作“金牕”，华美的窗。

⑤慵：同“庸”。困倦，懒。

Thanks for New Bestowing (3)

Guests left the empty courtyard to return,
The Painted Hall shut half with pearls curtain.
The grove wind blew softly at deep night.
The petty chamber is with crescent light,
Looking back, it is an elegant maiden.

Man would be aged as spring invisible light,
New sorrow and old hatred were endless.
Still sleepy, lazy to get up though windows bright.
Qiangdi Flute's song made a sudden surprise to her pink cheeks with a smile.

谢新恩
（樱花落尽阶前月）
（四）

樱花落尽阶前月，
象床愁倚薰笼。
远似去年今日，
恨还同。

双鬟不整云憔悴，
泪沾红抹胸[①]。
何处相思苦？
纱窗醉梦中。

Thanks for New Bestowing (4)

Cherry blossoms fell down gate steps of stone
under the glittering moon,
The maiden lay over the cage hung.
Recalling last year's today,
With the same melancholy in the same way.

Double sideburns in disorder,
She was haggard,
Tears shedding on her dress front.
Where's her lovesickness stronger?
Windows locked her bedroom,
She dreamed of screens' dream.

【译注】

①抹胸：肚兜。

谢新恩
（樱桃落尽春将困）
（五）

樱桃落尽春将困，
秋千架下归时。
漏[1]暗斜月迟迟，
花在枝。

（缺十二字）
彻晓纱窗下，
待来君不知。

Thanks for New Bestowing (5)

Cherry blossoms all faded away, spring sleepy,
The maiden returning back from her swing frame play.
The Water Clock* dim, the moon rising slantingly,
Over sprigs top of the flowery.

Via the window she saw the daybreak,
Waiting for the monarch.

【译注】

①漏：漏壶，古代计时之器。“漏水下百刻，以分昼夜。”

[Annotation]

*The Water Clock is an ancient timer was called "Lou" (In Chinese PININ) like a copper pot with a hole, through which water or very fine sands gradually to fall so as to engrave a marking to account time.

谢新恩
（冉冉秋光留不住）
（六）

冉冉[①]秋光留不住，
满阶红叶暮。
又是过重阳，
台榭登临处。

茱萸[②]香坠，
紫菊气，飘庭户，
晚烟笼细雨。
嗈嗈[③]新雁咽寒声，
愁恨年年长相似。

【译注】

①冉冉：柔软下垂地；慢慢地。

②茱萸：（dogwood；cornel，cornus）一种植物。

③嗈嗈 (yōng yōng)：鸟类和鸣声。

【译注】

清末民初学者刘继增（1843—1905）《南唐二主词笺》注云：此阕既不分段，亦不类本调，而他调亦无有似此填者。以上六词，原注谓出

Thanks for New Bestowing (6)

It’s impossible to stop the autumn rhyme to
flow,
No one can stop it to flow.
The stone steps full of leafs of maple.
It’s the Double Sun Festival,
To climb up the pavilion hill to seek for the
fragrant cornel.

The yard emitted chrysanthemum smell,
The evening scenery is of the hazy drizzle.
New wild geese whine,
As similar as maids’ melancholy sigh yearly
days and nights.

孟郡王家墨迹，疑当时纸幅断烂，录者谨依，错简如此。

【原注】

这首词据《历代诗余》注："单调，五十一字，止李煜一首，不分前后段，存以备体。"刘继增《南唐二主词笺》中也说它："既不分段，亦不类本调，而他调亦无有似此填者。"而依《词律拾遗》则作"补调"，其注曰："此词不分前后迭，疑有脱误。叶本（叶申芗《天籁轩词谱》）于'处'字分段。"依此说。

长相思

（云一緺）

云[1]一緺[2]，玉[3]一梭，
澹澹[4]衫儿薄薄罗。
轻颦双黛螺[5]。

秋风多，雨相和，
帘外芭蕉三两窠[6]。
夜长人奈何？

Long Lovesickness

It's a girl's hair-bun,
Decorating a hair-pin,
Like a jade-shuttle.
Her pretty shirt made of thin silk fabric,
She's frowning double eyebrows black.

The autumn wind blew strong,
The rain was accompanying on,
Outside the window curtain,
Two or three bananas stood in the rain.
At long night they remained lonely in vain.

【译注】

①云：鬓发。
②緺（wō）：像水流旋转盘结的发髻。
③玉：玉簪。
④澹澹（dàn dàn）：悠悠，轻轻舒卷。
⑤黛螺：别作“翠娥”，指代眉毛。
⑥窠：古同“棵”。

长相思
（一重山）

一重山，两重山。
山远天高烟水寒，
相思枫叶丹。

菊花开，菊花残。
塞雁高飞人未还，
一帘风月闲。

Long Lovesickness

One mountain high,
Two mountains wide,
Both of them are in far sight.
The sky is high,
To look at the misty cold creek.
The girl is lovesick,
Maple leafs timely in pink.

Now chrysanthemums bloom,
Then the withered await them.
The north wild geese fly high,
The sweetheart has not been back.
The flirting moon looks idly romantic.

捣练子令[1]
（深院静）

深院静，小庭空，
断续寒砧断续风。
无奈夜长人不寐，
数声和月到帘栊。

Pounding Clothes on Anvil

The deep courtyard is quiet inside,
The empty courtyard is small in size,
A stone anvil pounded intermittently with the wind noisy.
An uneasy man lay sleepless at night long.
The window emitted her anvil song with the moon along.

【译注】

①“捣练子”是词牌，练是一种白丝熟绢，须用木杵在砧石上捶击（捣）而成；令指小令，是短歌（此小令仅有二十七个字）。

捣练子令

（云鬟乱）

云鬟乱，晚妆残，
带恨眉儿远岫[1]攒[2]。
斜托香腮春笋嫩[3]，
为谁和泪倚阑干。

Pounding Clothes on Anvil

Her sideburns were in disorder but pretty gentle,
Her evening makeup was like an incomplete show,
Her melancholy eyebrows seemed to be far peaks,
One tender hand slantingly supported her cheeks.
Who could excite her to shed tears fully?
While leaning upon her railing voicelessly?

【译注】

①远岫（xiù）：远处的山峰。
②攒（cuán）：簇聚，凑集。这里指紧皱双眉。
③春笋嫩：以春笋的白、滑、细来比美人的纤纤素手。

阮郎归
呈郑王十二弟①

东风吹水日衔山，
春来长是闲。
落花狼藉酒阑珊②，
笙歌醉梦间。

佩声③悄，晚妆残，
凭谁整翠鬟④？
留连光景惜朱颜，
黄昏独倚阑。

Fancy Musician Returned
Dedicated to My Younger Brother King Zheng

The east wind was dancing over the river,
The sun was to swallow the hilltop,
The idle spring has lasted longer,
Withered flowers flied down in disorder,
The cup of wine still has not dried up,
The singing flute seemed tipsy in dream.

Her jade sound quiet, she was lazy in makeup,
Who attracted the maiden carefully to comb?
She'd treasure the vernal scenic season,
  but worry of fading away her face crimson.
At twilight, alone she leaned upon the door
  screen.

【译注】

①李煜弟李从善（940 年 ~ 987 年），李璟第七子，南唐时封郑王。开宝四年（971 年），前去朝贡宋太祖。该词当作于此时。

②阑珊：残尽。

③佩声：古人服饰环佩，行动时有声。

④整翠鬟：指梳头。

蝶恋花①

（遥夜亭皋闲信步）

遥夜②亭皋③闲信步，
乍过清明，
早觉④伤春暮。
数点雨声风约住⑤，
朦胧澹⑥月云来去。

桃李依依⑦春暗度。
谁在秋千，
笑里轻轻语。
一片芳心⑧千万绪，
人间没个安排处。

【译注】

①谁是此词真实作者，向有不同说法。一说是李冠，一说是李煜。若根据《全唐诗》等版本推断应是李煜。

②遥夜：长夜，深夜。

③皋（gāo）：水边地。

④早觉：《全唐诗》等本亦作“渐觉”。

⑤约住：指雨声被风声遮住。

⑥澹：清静。

⑦桃李：《尊前集》等本亦作“桃杏”。“桃李”形容人的容貌姣美。依依：形容鲜花盛开的样子。

⑧芳心：花蕊。这里指女人心。

Butterfly-Love-Flower

At midnight along the waterside kiosk,
Leisurely I went for a walk.
Just gone was the Memorial Day,
Gradually I grieved over spring fading away.
The louder wind lowered the drizzling tone,
Through clouds was the pale moon.

The peaches and plums reluctantly part with spring voicelessly vanishing.
Who was to play in swinging?
With a smile, lightly chatting?
One sweet heart could contain thousands of true affection,
The human world had no place to hold her love emotion.

临江仙
（樱桃落尽春归去）

樱桃落尽春归去，
蝶翻轻粉双飞。
子规啼月小楼西，
玉钩罗幕，
惆怅暮烟垂。

门巷寂寥人散后，
望残烟草低迷。
炉香闲袅凤凰儿[①]。
空持罗带[②]，
回首恨依依。

【译注】
①凤凰儿：指衾枕上的彩饰。
②罗带：亦作“裙带”，喻指小周后。

Riverside Fairy Maiden

Spring returned with all the falling-down cherry,
Butterflies and light pollens were to fly mutually.
The cuckoo sang to the moon over the mansion,
The jade hooks hooked up the west-chamber curtain,
My melancholy immersed into the twilight.

Along the lonely lane, no one walking on foot,
Grass was seen sluggish in the misty light.
The censer smoke was idle to curl around her phoenix-pillow.
She held her silk belt vainly in sorrow to look back lingering love not long ago.

临江仙
（补李后主词）

樱桃结子春归尽，
蝶翻金粉双飞。
子规啼月小楼西。
玉钩罗幕，
惆怅卷金泥。

门巷寂寥人去后，
望残烟草低迷。
（上为后主词）
何时重听玉骢[①]嘶。
扑帘飞絮，
依约梦回时[②]。

【译注】

①骢（cōng）：青白色的马。

②最后三句为后人所加。

Riverside Fairy Maiden

Spring returned with all the falling-down cherry,
Butterflies and light pollens were to fly mutually.
The cuckoo sang to the moon over the mansion,
The jade hooks hooked up the west-chamber curtain,
My melancholy rolled up golden twilight.

Along the lonely lane, no one walking on foot,
Grass was seen sluggish in the misty light.
When to listen to young horse to neigh again?
When flying catkins toward my curtain?
Seemingly I dreamed of my dream to return.

破阵子
（四十年来家国）

四十年来家国，
三千里地山河。
凤阁龙楼连霄汉，
玉树琼枝作烟萝。
几曾识干戈！

一旦归为臣虏，
沈腰潘鬓[①]消磨。
最是仓皇辞庙日，
教坊犹奏别离歌。
垂泪对宫娥。

Breakthrough Battle Array

It's my homeland with forty-year history,
With 3000-km mountain-and-river territory.
Dragon-phoenix style pavilions link with the Milky Way,
Jadelike trees with everlasting long twigs seem misty.
Fighting by sword never suited my character!

Yet once got as an official captive member,
He would turn lean, haggard with gray hair.
It's extremely farewell to ancestral temple,
Imperial musicians played a song of farewell.
Tears dropped toward maidens of the palace hall.

【译注】

①沈腰潘鬓：南朝梁沈约老病，百余日中，腰带数移孔；又晋潘岳年始三十二岁，即生白发。后人以“沈腰潘鬓”为典故，形容身体消瘦，头发斑白。

乌夜啼[1]

（林花谢了春红）

林花谢了春红，太匆匆。
无奈朝来寒雨晚来风。

胭脂泪[2]，相留醉，几时重[3]。
自是人生长恨水长东。

【译注】

①此词牌调原为唐教坊曲，又名《相见欢》《秋夜月》《上西楼》。三十六字，上片平韵，下片两仄韵两平韵。

②胭脂泪：女子脸上搽有胭脂，泪水流经脸颊时沾上胭脂的红色。

③几时重：何时再度相会。

Crows Cry at Night

Spring red blossoms faded away too quickly.
To stop morning rain or evening wind is not easy.

Girls' tears let boys tipsy,
When will we meet?
Long life with long regret,
Is like water flowing to east.

相见欢①
（无言独上西楼）

无言独上西楼，
月如钩。
寂寞梧桐深院锁清秋。

剪不断，
理还乱，
是离愁。
别是一番滋味在心头。

Joyful Reunion

Upstairs, voicelessly I'd like to go,
The moon is like a bow.
The deep courtyard can hold,
Lonely parasol tree to lock autumn cold.

It is impossible to cut off my sorrow,
I comb it up but fail,
No way to cancel my parting sorrow.
In my heart it's a tasteful farewell.

【译注】

①此词牌一名《乌夜啼》。

[Annotation]

Indus, phoenix tree, parasol tree or Chinese parasol used to denote to the same tree. As a new word, indus can be understood by Google Translation.

乌夜啼
（昨夜风兼雨）

昨夜风兼雨，
帘帏飒飒秋声。
烛残漏断频欹[1]枕，
起坐不能平。

世事漫随流水，
算来一梦浮生[2]。
醉乡路稳宜频到，
此外不堪行。

【译注】

①欹：通“倚”，斜倚。

②浮生：人生在世，虚浮不定。《庄子》：“其生若浮，其死若休。”

Crows Cry at Night

Last night it's heard of wind and rain,
My tent and curtain locked the sough autumn.
The candle's residual, Water Clock stopped to go,
Repeatedly I leaned upon my pillow,
I was uneasy to adjust it high or low.

Everything goes on like water in flow,
To sum up, my whole life is only a dream.
The tipsy fairyland is as security as home,
Other road is impossible to reach my aim.

望江梅
（闲梦远）

闲梦远，南国正芳春。
船上管弦江面绿[1]，
满城飞絮滚轻尘，
忙杀看花人。

Looking over the South Riverside

My leisurely dream going far away,
The south land is on lush spring day.
On the river boat Pipa heard to play,
The whole city is full of light catkins,
All the flower-loving men are busy.

【译注】

①绿：也作“渌”。指水清，清澈。

望江梅
（闲梦远）

闲梦远，南国正清秋。
千里江山寒色远，
芦花深处泊孤舟，
笛在月明楼。

Looking over the South Riverside

My dream going far away,
The south land is on clear autumn day.
Myriad rivers and mountains out or stop cold way,
The lonely boat mooring at the thick reed lake,
The Bright Moon Kiosk heard of short flute music.

望江南①（多少恨）

多少恨，昨夜梦魂中。
还似旧时游上苑，
车如流水马如龙。
花月正春风。

Looking over the South Riverside

How much hatred hidden in my dream last night?
The scenery is still of the past sight.
Carts ran as if water were flowing,
The horses gallop as if dragons dancing.
Under the vernal moon, flowers were blooming.

【译注】

①两首《望江南》（多少恨 / 多少泪）均为南唐亡国归宋时之作，追念昔日故国繁盛，抒发今日亡国凄清。《望江南》原名《谢秋娘》，唐李德裕谢秋娘之作。白居易根据词末句“能不忆江南”改名《忆江南》，温庭筠又易名为《望江南》。李煜词中的《望江南》《望江梅》为同一词调。

望江南
（多少泪）

多少泪，断脸复横颐[①]。
心事莫将和泪说，
凤笙[②]休向泪时吹，
肠断更无疑。

Looking over the South Riverside

How many tears shed over your cheeks?
Don't talk your mind in shedding tears,
Don't play phoenix-sheng flute to tearful face,
That must be heartbroken in sadness.

【译注】

①横颐：颐，指脸颊。全句意为泪水纵横交流。

②凤笙：笙长四寸、十二簧，像凤之身，称“凤笙”。

虞美人①
（风回小院庭芜绿）

风回小院庭芜绿，
柳眼[2]春相续。
凭阑半日独无言，
依旧竹声新月似当年。

笙歌未散尊罍[3]在，
池面冰初解。
烛明香暗画堂深，
满鬓清霜残雪思难任[4]。

Beautiful Lady Yu

The returned breeze warms small yard weeds in green,
The spring willows have been continuously awoken.
I am silently lonely,
leaning upon balustrade half a day,
The crescent moon still shines as the past days.

With the wind, bamboos make much noise,
The Sheng-flute in playing, wine cups remain,
The pool's ice is melt initially.
The candles bright, incenses dim,
Deeply secluded is the inside room.
My sideburns turn grey,
I could not tolerate melancholy.

【译注】

①《虞美人》，原为唐教坊曲，此调因初咏项羽宠姬虞美人得名。又名《一江春水》《玉壶冰》《巫山十二峰》等。双调，五十六字，上下片各四句，皆为两仄韵转两平韵。

②柳眼：早春时柳树初生的嫩叶，好像人的睡眼初展，故称柳眼。李商隐《二月二日》诗中有"花须柳眼多无赖，紫蝶黄蜂俱有情"之句。又元稹《寄浙西李大夫》（四首之一），也有"柳眼梅心渐欲春"的诗句。

③尊罍（léi）：酒杯。

④难任：难以承受。

虞美人
（春花秋月何时了）

春花秋月何时了，
往事知多少！
小楼昨夜又东风，
故国不堪回首月明中。

雕栏玉砌应犹在，
只是朱颜改。
问君能有几多愁？
恰似一江春水向东流。

Beautiful Lady Yu

What time spring flowers will no longer bloom ?
And the autumn moon will not shine in the dome?
How many events took place?
Who knows?
The east wind blew my chamber last night,
I recalled my motherland in the moonlight.

Standing still's my palace jade-like railing of marble,
Yet my ruddy face looked changeable.
Were to ask how much of your sorrow?
That's exactly like the spring river to flow.

[Annotation]

(1)The title with double square brackets (mark < >) refers to Verse Ci （something like an English word concept, Lyrics） or Qu tune name , which is an ancient music title.

(2) As a lyrics, it would be sung according to its tune,which is quite different from each other in melody. Such lyrics should be written to suit some tune with strict tonal patterns and rhyme schemes, in fixed verse lines and words. Ci-Verse or Lyrics originated in the Tang Dynasty (618 ～ 907) and further developed in the Song Dynasty (960 ～ 1279).

浪淘沙
（往事只堪哀）

往事只堪哀，
对景难排。
秋风庭院藓侵阶。
一桁[1]珠帘闲不卷，
终日谁来。

金剑[2]已沉埋，
壮气蒿莱。
晚凉天净月华开。
想得玉楼瑶殿影，
空照秦淮。

Billows Washing the Sand

It is worth to recall my sorrow,
Though releasing grief is difficult,
  to face her lonely shadow.
In the courtyard, the autumn wind blows,
On the marble steps, green mosses grow.
The idle beaded curtains roll down,
Who will be to come here along?

My golden sword was hidden in ground,
My will camouflaged into the wormwood.
I imagine the jade chamber of paradise,
The silent sky is covering the cool night with
  the moonlight,
Vainly to shine over Qinhuai.

【译注】

①一桁（héng）：（名）檩。窗框等上的横木。有的版本，一桁亦作“一任”。

② 金剑：一说“金锁”，或“金敛”，疑是误传。

浪淘沙
（帘外雨潺潺）

帘外雨潺潺，
春意阑珊。
罗衾不耐五更寒。
梦里不知身是客，
一晌贪欢。

独自莫凭栏，
无限江山。
别时容易见时难。
流水落花春去也，
天上人间。

Billows Washing the Sand

It's drizzling outside my curtain,
Spring in the air is waning again.
The silk quilt couldn't keep me night warm.
I don't know I'm a captive bird in my dream,
I try to have it as happy as home.

Don't be lonely to lean upon balustrade,
Looking over the boundless vast land.
That's easy lost but hard got.
With the running water,
Fallen flowers would flow.
Spring vanished on the go.
My heyday empire no longer,
Like human paradise time ago.

子夜歌
（人生愁恨何能免）

人生愁恨何能免？
销魂①独我情何限②！
故国梦重归，
觉③来双泪垂。

高楼谁与上④？
长记秋晴望⑤。
往事已成空，
还如一梦中。

Midnight Song

In life, hatred and sorrow will happen.
No limit to release my lonely ecstasy without pain!
I dreamed of my homeland back again,
Awoken, my double eyes' tears fallen.

Who'd be upstairs with me for overlooking?
On an autumn sunny day, I recall far sightseeing.
All the past events were gone with nothing,
As if still dreaming.

【译注】

①销魂：灵魂离开肉体。此处意为极度愁苦，亦可用来形容极度快乐。
②何限：哪里有个边际。
③觉：醒。
④谁与上：与谁上。
⑤秋晴望：在秋日的晴空下登高远望。

三台令

（不寐倦长更）

不寐倦长更，
披衣出户行。
月寒秋竹冷，
风切夜窗声。

Three-Pavilion Short Lyric Verse

Sleepless, I am tired of long night,
I put on my overcoat to go out.
The moon is cold, the autumn bamboos frosty,
The night wind penetrates the window, noisy.

【译注】

唐教坊曲中有大曲《三台》。据唐刘禹锡《嘉话录》云："邺中有曹公铜雀、金虎、冰井三台，北齐高洋毁之更筑金凤、圣应、崇光三台，宫人拍呼上台送酒，因名其曲为《三台》。"词牌有"令"字者一般为短小曲调。

开元乐①
（心事数茎白发）

心事数②茎白发，
生涯一片青山。
空林③有雪相待，
野路④无人自还⑤。

Establishing-New-Dynasty Music

A few stems of grey hair show my mind in pain,
My sophisticated career is like a green mountain.
In the empty forest, snow is waiting for me,
On the wild path, no one but I home again.

【译注】

①开元乐：词牌名，又名“翠华引”。

②数：清刻本《诗人玉屑》中作“千”。

③空林：指人烟罕至，幽深的山林。詹安泰《李璟李煜词》《南唐二主词汇笺》等本中均作“空山”。

④野路：村野间的田间小路。《万首唐人绝句》《东坡题跋》《诗话总龟》前六卷中均作“古路”。

⑤自还：独自行走。《万首唐人绝句》《东坡题跋》《诗话总龟》前六卷中均作“独还”。

浣溪沙
（转烛飘蓬一梦归）

转烛①飘蓬②一梦归，
欲寻陈迹③怅④人非，
天教心愿与身违。

待月⑤池台⑥空逝水，
荫花⑦楼阁漫斜晖，
登临不惜更沾衣。

【译注】

①转烛：风吹烛火。
②飘蓬：飘动的蓬草，比喻人世沧桑，漂泊不定。
③陈迹：过去事遗留的痕迹。
④怅：怅惘，不如意。
⑤待月：暗指月夜情人约会。
⑥池台：池苑楼台。
⑦荫花：《全唐诗》中作“映花”。荫，隐藏，遮挡。

Washing-Creek-Sand

As candle glistening unsteadily, an old dream returned again,
I was melancholy to dream of no residual traces of the maiden,
It’s God to intend to violate our affectionate reunion desire.

Only we could watch creek flow under the moonlight,
The pretty pavilion shrouded by the flowery shadow,
Upstairs to the top, I shed tears with deep sorrow.

柳枝①
（赐宫人庆奴）

风情②渐老见春羞，
到处销魂感旧游。
多谢③长条似相识，
强垂烟态拂人头。

Weeping Willow Twigs
Dedicated to imperial palace maiden Qingnu

My affection weak, I am shy to see you spring girl,
Everywhere I release my soul to feel past travel.
I would like to be grateful to the weeping willow,
With a nod, long twigs wave hello to the people.

【译注】

①此词调名于诸本二主词或作《柳枝》，或作《杨柳枝》。这首词于清《全唐诗》中有题作“赐宫人庆奴”。

②风情：风月之情，男女相亲相爱之情，秀美容颜。

③多谢：一作“多见”。

柳枝

（风情渐老见春羞）

风情渐老见春羞，
到处芳魂感旧游。
多谢长条似相识，
强垂烟穗拂人头。

Weeping Willow Twigs

Spring amorous style let me feel old and shameful,
Everything lush let me recall the past too beautiful.
Thank for the weeping willow twigs as I know,
You scatter catkins over our heads to flow.

后庭花破子①
（玉树后庭前）

玉树后庭前，
瑶草妆镜边。
去年花不老，
今年月又圆。

莫教偏②，
和月和花，
天教长少年。

Courtyard Flowers

In front of courtyard, a jade-like tree standing still,
Her mirror edge decorated by pearl-grass immortal.
Last year the blooming blossoms grew still youthful,
This year the crescent moon hovers to look still full.

Do not complain about my prejudice,
Toward the moon,
Toward the blossom,
The heaven still favors you as well as the juvenile.

【译注】

①破子：曲调，大曲或联章的尾声结曲。（一为双调53字，一为双调50字。）

这首词是李煜写给娥皇大周后的。娥皇曾因发现自己妹妹，即小周后与李煜调情而倍受打击，又因爱子仲宣的突然病逝更加绝望，身体更加虚弱，不久就谢世了，李煜因为内疚也加深了对娥皇的思念，于是便写下了这首诗；将娥皇比作后宫庭院里高贵的玉树、梳妆台镜边的仙草，李煜寄希望于良辰美景，花好月圆，永远和娥皇为伴，用花好月圆作比，抒发青春永驻的美好心愿。笔走龙蛇，浑然一体，出手不凡，绘出了天人自然合一的境地。（有学者说该词是冯延巳或元好问所作。）

②偏：偏怜，偏爱。“莫教偏，和月和花，天教长少年”大意是“不要让这一切有变化！请让青春年少，如同这花月一般永驻”。

更漏[1]子
（金雀钗）

（一说温庭筠作）

金雀钗，红粉面，花里暂时相见。
知我意，感君怜，此情须问天。

香作穗[2]，蜡成泪，还似两人心意。
珊枕腻[3]，锦衾寒，觉来更漏残。

Night Water Clock

The pink-cheeked girl with a gold-bird hairpin,
She stood up in flowers eagerly once to be seen.
Understanding her intention was a man,
For whom thanks should be given.

The heaven might know such affection,
Incense burnt into ash spike near the tearful candle,
The tearful drops seemed their love symbol.
Embroidery quilt was cold, with a cool coral pillow,
At dead night, clock's residual water was still in flow.

【译注】

①更：旧时夜间计时的单位，一夜分为五更。更漏：原指计时用的漏壶，后泛指时辰。

②香作穗：燃烧着的香生成的烟凝聚不散成穗状。宋苏舜钦有“香穗萦斜凝画栋”的描写。

③珊枕：指以珊瑚制作或装饰的枕头。别作“山枕”，即珊瑚枕。唐代李绅有“珊瑚枕上千行泪”。珊枕腻：此指滑而不能着枕。

更漏子
（柳丝长）

（一说温庭筠作）

柳丝长，春雨细，花外漏声迢递[①]。
惊塞雁，起城乌，画屏金鹧鸪。

香雾薄，透重幕，惆怅谢家[②]池阁。
红烛背，绣帏垂，梦长君不知。

Night Water Clock

The willow sprigs long, spring drizzle lingering on,
Outside flowers, Clock's water flowing down.
The wild geese fly, crows call, francolins paint on the screen.

The fragrant mist is thin, through the heavy curtain,
Melancholy shrouded Xie-family* waterside pavilion.
The red candle faint, embroidery curtain vertical,
Her dream long, her sweetheart did not know.

【译注】

①迢递（tiáo dì）：遥远。

②谢家：指东晋谢安家。常用以代称高门世族之家。

[Annotation]

*Xie here refers to Prime Ministers, namely, Xie An in the East Jin Dynasty (317 ~ 420).

南歌子①
（云鬓裁新绿）

云鬓裁②新绿，
霞衣③曳④晓红。
待歌凝立翠筵中，
一朵彩云⑤何事下巫峰⑥。

趁拍⑦鸾飞镜⑧，
回身燕漾空。
莫翻红袖过帘栊⑨，
怕被杨花⑩勾引嫁东风。

The Southern Singing Girl

Sideburns inserted of new green decoration,
Her rosy-cloud dress allured the morning sun.
To wait for singing, she stood upon the mattress,
Why did she turn colorful clouds like a goddess
flying out of the Wu-Peaks?

Welcome such a bird-like a girl in the mirror's
shadow,
As if a swallow was flying within the curtain-
window.
Not to expose her red sleeves, she feared catkins
lure the east wind to marry her well.

【译注】

①《南唐二主词》辑录了此词，认为从词意上看，当是李煜前期的作品，排除了此词为苏轼之作一说。

②裁：这里指插戴。

③霞衣：指舞蹈时穿的霞帔。

④曳（yè）：拖，拉。

⑤彩云：绚丽多彩的云朵。这里指巫山神女。

⑥巫峰：即巫山，用巫山神女比喻舞女的光彩照人。

⑦趁拍：合着节拍。

⑧鸾飞镜：即鸾镜。指化妆时用的镜子。

⑨栊（lóng）：窗户。

⑩杨花：也指柳絮。

青玉案①

（梵宫百尺同云护）

梵宫②百尺同云护，
渐白满苍苔路。
破腊③梅花李蚤露④。
银涛无际，玉山万里，
寒罩江南树。

鸦啼影乱天将暮，
海月纤痕映烟雾。
修竹低垂孤鹤舞。
杨花风弄，鹅毛天剪，
总是诗人误。

【译注】

①明代潘游龙《古今诗余醉》中记述这首词是李后主所作。

②梵宫：原指梵天的宫殿，后多指佛寺。

③破腊：指的是阴历腊月初八。

④李：李花。蚤：通“早”。破腊梅花李蚤露：全句的意思是“眼前虽然是腊八节气，但梅花、李花的花蕾早已吐露出来”。

Blue-Jade Tea Tray

Clouds shroud the 100-foot-high Vatican
Palace,
The white mist hover the desolate mossy path.
On Dec. 8 festival, plums in bloom full of
dews.
The boundless sight is of silver-white snow,
The longest scenery is of jade-mountain row,
Coldness covers trees along the south river
bank.

The disorderly crows cry for it will be at dusk,
The gentle sea moonlight shines in the misty
air.
The bamboos seem to dance in crane manner.
The wind is playing with the catkins,
As if swan feathers were cut off by the
heaven,
Poets may be misunderstood by such scene.

秋霁

虹影侵阶，乍雨歇长空，万里凝碧。
孤鹜高飞，落霞相映，远状水乡秋色。
黯然望极。
动人无限愁如织。
又听得。
云外数声，新雁正嘹呖[①]。

After an Autumn Rain

The rainbow shadow lies on the doorstep outside,
The abrupt rain stops to rest in the azure sky,
The clear blue space expands for 10000 miles.
One lonely wild duck is to fly,
The rosy clouds are falling in twilight,
The water village afar is an autumn sight.
I am dejected to watch the endless goal,
Unlimitedly excitable with deep sorrow.
I heard also,
Of new wild geese to call as clouds flow.

当此暗想，画阁轻抛，杳然殊无，些个消息。
漏声稀，银屏冷落，那堪残月照窗白。
衣带顿宽犹阻隔。
算此情苦，除非宋玉[②]风流，共怀伤感，有谁知得。

Then I imagined the painted pavilion,
To be thrown lightly to the heaven,
With no special sight,
Just few vague outlines to provide.
The water-clock sounds light.
The silver screen is desolate,
Unable to let the waning crescent to shine over the window in white.
I look lean and haggard without reunion,
I am bitter with lovesick affection,
Unless Song Yu's flirtatious ability,
With the same melancholy,
Who knows me?

【译注】

①嘹呖（liáo lì）：形容声音响亮凄清。[例句]哀彼中泽鸿，嘹呖号寒冰。

②宋玉：（公元前298年—？）又名子渊，楚国辞赋作家。屈原弟子。

残词（1~2）

（1）

别易会难无可奈。

【译注】

据宋代吴曾《能改斋漫录》第16卷“别易会难条”条，录有《颜氏家训》的说法：李后主长短句用过“别易会难无可奈”；但颜说又有《文选》云：“分索则易，携手实难。”据此，让人相信引证李煜话者亦难。

（2）

细雨湿流光。

【译注】

出自《雪浪斋日记》荆公与山谷对话——山谷以为“细雨湿流光”是出自李煜的词。实际上，此句为南唐冯延巳《南乡子》首句。

Few Poetic Lines Doubtfully Considered as Residual Works (1~2)

(1)

Easy to separate,
Difficult to reunite again,
Which is helpless to complain.

[Annotation]

As one of the so-called “residual poetic sentences” it is considered as one of Emperor Li Yu’s works, but in fact there may be something wrong because two authoritive classic books provided the text being not exactly the same words, therefore it was controversial.

(2)

The lingering drizzle had wetted passing years.

[Annotation]

In fact, this residual poetic sentence was not originated from Li Yu’s works. It was the first poetic line of Feng Yanshi’s poem.

Feng Yansi (903~960) was once appointed as Primary Minister and invited as an imperial teacher teaching prince Li Yu (937~978).

南乡子

细雨湿流光，
芳草年年与恨长。
烟锁凤楼无限事，
茫茫。
鸾镜鸳衾两断肠。

魂梦任悠扬，
睡起杨花满绣床。
薄悻不来门半掩，
斜阳。
负你残春泪几行。

Township South Man

Drizzle wetted my flowing time ago,
Yearly along with hatred, sweet grass grow.
The mist locked the love story,
In the Pheonix Pavilion,
Under the vast heaven.
I look at my makeup mirror,
And embroidery quilt cover.
I felt heartbroken and lovesick.

My soul dream was romantic.
Sleepless, I lay on my bed,
With full catkins flying over.
The fickle guy has not clicked,
My lonely half-open door,
Till the setting sun not tall.
To repay the residual spring,
A few lines of my tears fall.

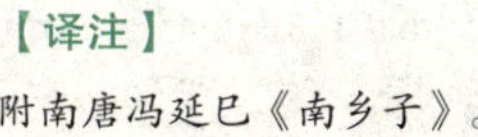

【译注】

附南唐冯延巳《南乡子》。

失调名

楼上春寒水四面。[①]
"风乍起、吹皱一池春水"。[②]
"桃李不须夸烂熳，已输了春风一半"。[③]

【译注】

宋代江休复所撰《江邻几杂志》卷上（《星凤阁校录》）山谷《茶磨铭》有记载：①李后主於清微殿歌"楼上春寒水四面"，②学士刁衎起奏："风乍起、吹皱一池春水。"③韩熙载和云："桃李不须夸烂熳，已输了春风一半。"

此记载反映了李煜与内臣议政也少不了用诗词对话的习惯。

【刁衎】（945—1013），字元宾。李后主时韩熙载任学士承旨（官名），刁衎为一（翰林）学士。《宋史》卷441有传，《全宋诗》录了他四首诗。

【韩熙载】（902—970）五代十国南唐时期大臣、文学家。后主李煜时期，曾任兵部尚书，充勤政殿学士承旨等要职（相当于执行首相或内相）。他目睹国势日蹙，身处疑难，遂广蓄女乐，彻夜宴饮以排遣忧愤。《韩熙载夜宴图》是五代十国南唐画家顾闳中作品，是中国十大传世名画之一。

The Title Lost

Upstairs spring chill moat surrounds all sides.
(Courtier Diao:)
Suddenly wind began to ripple a pond of spring.
(Courtier Han:)
No need to praise briliant peaches and plums,
As their beauty being stolen a half by spring breeze.

[Annotation]

"Jiang Xiufu's Several Magazines" (the front volume) recorded a dialogue between Emperor Li Yu and his two imperial academicians as follows:

① Li Yu: Upstairs spring chill moat surrounds all sides.

② Diao Yan: Suddenly wind began to ripple a pond of spring.

③ Han Xizai: No need to praise briliant peaches and plums, as their beauty being stolen a half by spring breeze.

This record reflects customary that Li Yu and and his courtiers used to make a dialogue in poetic words.

第三部分

Part Three

（一）英译南唐中主李璟诗词全集（7首）

（二）英译南唐先主李昪唯一传世之诗

游后湖赏莲花

蓼花蘸水火不灭，
水鸟惊鱼银梭投。
满目荷花千万顷，
红碧相杂敷清流。
孙武已斩吴宫女，
琉璃池上佳人头。

Appreciate Lake Lotuses

The vine-flower with water like burning fire,
Osprey let silver-shuttle fish surprised.
My eyes full of lotuses float on the vast water,
The red and the green cover the clear river.
Lotus crowns seemed to be cut by Army men,
As if the Crystal Lake sealed by heads of maiden.

【译注】

原文出处：《全唐诗》卷八并参照清代王国维辑本《南唐二主词》。

李璟 (916 ~ 961)：徐州（今江苏徐州）人。十岁，起官驾部郎中。十五岁，为兵部尚书参知政事。升元元年 (937)，封吴王。保大元年 (943)，先主李昪卒，嗣位为南唐皇帝。交泰元年 (958)，兵败于后周，遂去帝号，称国主，在位十九年，庙号元宗，又称中主。

登楼赋

保大五年元日大雪同太弟景遂、汪王景逖、齐王景達、进士李建勋、中书徐铉、勤政殿学士张义方登楼赋。

珠帘高卷莫轻遮，
往往相逢隔岁华。
春气昨宵飘律管，
东风今日放梅花。
素姿好把芳姿掩，
落势还同舞势斜。
坐有宾朋樽有酒，
可怜清味属侬家。

Intone Going Upstairs

It was a heavy snow day, on January 1, 947, younger brother Li Jingsui, King-Wang Li Jingdi, King-Qi Li Jingkui, Jinshi Li Jianxun (high official candidate of imperial examination), Courtier Xu Xuan and Imperial Academy's member Zhang Yifang as well as I went upstairs to intone the following poem.

Roll bead-curtain up high, let far-sight not be hidden,
Usually long time passed, reunion will happen again.
Last night flute music floating in spring air dome,
Today east wind blows plum blossoms to bloom.
White flowery posture will cover colorful posture,
Flowers fall off dancing twigs in a slant manner.
Revered guests being seated, cups were full of wine,
It's a pity there was no enough tasteful food of mine.

句

灵槎[1]思浩荡，
老鹤倚崆峒。

苍苔迷古道，
红叶乱朝霞。

栖凤枝梢犹软弱，
化龙形状已依稀。

One Sentence, One Poem

Boarding a legend boat won rich vast imagination,
An old crane settled down on a kongtong mountain.

Luxuriant mosses cover an ancient road,
Red maple leafs mistaken for the rosy cloud.

The wind settling down in twigs seem soft lean,
Changing into a dragon form to be vaguely seen.

【译注】

①灵槎：亦作“灵查”。能乘往天河的船筏。

应天长[1]

一钩初月临妆镜，
蝉鬓[2]凤钗慵不整[3]。
重帘[4]静，
层楼迥[5]，
惆怅[6]落花风不定。

柳堤芳草径，
梦断辘轳[7]金井[8]。
昨夜更阑[9]酒醒，
春愁过却病。

Reply to the Everlasting Heaven

Crescent-like brows appear in the mirror,
Her sideburns with hairpins not in good order.
Silk curtains all quiet.
The lofty pavilion let man disconsolate,
Flowers falling, the wind is to hesitate.

The fragrant grass path along the willow dam,
I was dreaming of a windlass well dream.
Last mid-night, I sobered from being drunk,
Without spring sorrow, however I was sick.

【译注】

①应天长：应，回应、响应之意。该词牌又名《应天长令》《应天长慢》。此调有小令、长调两体。

②蝉鬓：古代妇女的一种发式。两鬓薄如蝉翼。

③慵不整：懒散，无心梳洗。

④重帘：一层层帘幕。

⑤层楼：高楼。迥（jiǒng）：遥远，僻远。

⑥惆怅：因失意或失望而伤感、懊恼。

⑦辘轳：亦作“辘盘”，井上汲水的起重装置。比喻心中情思如辘轳般反复上下。

⑧金井：井栏上有雕饰的井。南朝梁·费昶《行路难》诗之一：“惟闻哑哑城上乌，玉栏金井牵辘轳。”

⑨更阑：更深夜残。

望远行

碧砌花光锦绣明，
朱扉长日镇长扃。
余寒不去梦难成，
炉香烟冷自亭亭。

辽阳月[①]，秣陵[②]砧，
不传消息但传情。
黄金窗下忽然惊，
征人归日二毛生[③]。

【译注】

①辽阳月：辽阳地区有衍水，即太子河经过，曾是秦始皇为报荆轲刺秦王之仇而追捕燕国太子丹的地方。诗人用辽阳月是发思古丧胆之幽怨。

②秣陵：对金陵（南京）的贬称。

③二毛生：长出了白发。

Look Afar

The green made flower bright as embroidery,
The red door was shut by a long bolt all the day.
Residual coldness made me dream of no dream,
In the censer, incenses in cold smoke stood firm.

The timid moon, Moling* anvil-sound high,
To pass on no news but affectionate sigh.
Under the wedding window, the girl surprised suddenly,
Her soldier-lover's hair turns grey on such a happy day.

[Annotation]

*Moling is a derogatory term for Jinling (i.e Nanking or Nanjing).

摊破①浣溪沙

（手卷真珠上玉钩）

手卷真珠上玉钩，
依前春恨锁重楼。
风里落花谁是主，
思悠悠。

青鸟不传云外信，
丁香空结雨中愁。
回首绿波三楚暮，
接天流。

【译注】

①摊破：亦称“添字”(浣溪沙)，实为《浣溪沙》之别体，不过多了三字两结句，移其韵于结句而已，因有“添字”“摊破”之名。

在《浣溪沙》或《摊破浣溪沙》这一词牌下李璟填了四首词，加上另外三首，李璟实际存词总数为七首、诗四首，其诗词一共应是十一首。

Longer Washing-Creek-Sand

To hang upon a jade-hook, she was rolling up a bead curtain.
In spring sorrow, maiden locked the door of her inside mansion.
Who was a master of falling flowers in the wind going on,
Her lovesickness lasted long.

The fairy blue bird passing on no news out of the heaven,
Cloves collected all the human sorrow in the lingering rain.
Looking back at the green waves of the Three-Chu twilight,
Wave upon wave, water seemed to link the Milky-Way sight.

摊破浣溪沙
（菡萏香销翠叶残）

菡萏[1]香销翠叶残，
西风愁起绿波间。
还与容光共憔悴，
不堪看。

细雨梦回鸡塞远，
小楼吹彻玉笙寒。
多少泪珠何限恨，
倚阑干。

Longer Washing-Creek-Sand

Lotus fragrance lost with green leafs residual,
On green waves, the west wind blew with sorrow.
Still mutually haggard with the time golden,
Heartbroken to see the scene.

In drizzling, dreaming of the frontier more remote,
A petty pavilion's full of music by a cool jade flute.
How many teardrops showed how much hatred,
Alone I leaned upon a balustrade.

【译注】

①菡萏（hàn dàn）：芙蓉、莲花、荷花的代称。

咏灯

一点分明值万金，
开时惟怕冷风侵。
主人若也勤挑拨，
敢向尊前不尽心。

【译注】

李昪（biàn）（888—943）：南唐烈祖，徐州彭城（今江苏徐州）人。五代十国时期南唐建立者。公元937年即位，在位七年。

Ode to Lamp

A little bit light is worth a priceless gold-coin,
Only afraid of the wind as you light it to open.
If it were frequently fiddled for being brighter,
It dares to be behaving in a careless manner.

[Annotation]

Li Bian (888 ~ 943) was the South-Tang's last emperor Li Yu's grandfather who was a founder of the South-Tang as one independent state during the Five Dynasties and Ten Kingdoms Period. Li Bian ascended the throne in 937 AD and had reigned for seven years.

附　录

（1）李煜年表（937～978）

937年（后晋天福二年/南唐升元元年）1岁，8月15日（农历七月初七），李煜生。

954年（后周显德元年/南唐保大十二年）18岁，娶娥皇。

958年（后周显德五年/南唐中兴元年）22岁，长子仲寓出生。

959年（后周显德六年）23岁，九月，太子弘冀卒，李煜自郑王徙封吴王。

961年（北宋建隆二年）25岁，二月，立为太子；七月，继位于金陵；尊母钟氏为圣尊后，立娥皇为皇后；遣使如宋表陈袭位；次子仲宣生于此年。

962年（北宋建隆三年）26岁，三月，遣使赴宋朝贡；六月，遣使赴宋朝贡；十一月，遣使赴宋朝贡。

963年（北宋乾德元年）27岁，三月，宋平荆南，遣使犒师；十一月，宋改元乾德。

964年（北宋乾德二年）28岁，三月，始行铁钱；十月，次子仲宣卒；十一月，皇后娥皇卒，亲撰《昭惠周后诔》。

965年（北宋乾德三年）29岁，正月，葬昭惠后于懿陵；四月，宋灭蜀，贡银绢以万计；九月，母圣尊后钟氏卒。

966年（北宋乾德四年）30岁，奉赵匡胤命，约南汉俱宋事，未成，将南汉回书呈宋。宋始决意伐南汉。

968年（北宋开宝元年）32岁，南唐旱灾；六月，遣弟从谦赴宋朝贡；十一月，娶小周后并立为皇后。

969年（北宋开宝二年）33岁，校猎青龙山，录囚大理寺，诸郡普度僧尼。

971年（北宋开宝四年）35岁，遣弟从谦入宋，贡珍宝数倍于前；十月，遣弟从善入宋朝贡；上表请去南唐国号，印文改为江南国，自称江南国主。

972年（北宋开宝五年）36岁，正月，贬损仪制，改诏为教，穿紫袍见宋；闰二月，宋留从善为泰宁军节度使，于汴梁建礼贤馆，待李煜降。

973年（北宋开宝七年）37岁，上表愿受宋爵命，宋朝不许；杀名将林仁肇。

974年（北宋开宝七年）38岁，上表宋，求从善归国，宋朝不许；遣使诏李煜入朝，不行，遂伐南唐。

975年（北宋开宝八年）39岁，宋军攻占金陵城关；三月，吴越兵攻常州，守将降；六月，宋军与吴越兵围困金陵，赵匡胤谕降；十一月二十七日，城破，李煜率子弟及官属4人出降。随宋将曹彬北上汴梁。南唐亡。

976年（北宋太平兴国元年）40岁，正月，受封为右千牛卫上将军、违命侯；十一月，进封陇西公。

978年（北宋太平兴国三年）42岁，七月八日，被赵光义毒死，追封为吴王；十月，以王礼葬于北邙山；小周后亦卒于此年，与李煜同葬。

Li Yu Chronology (937～978)

937 AD Li Yu was born on July 7 （lunar calendar） or August 15, 937 AD

It was the first year of Shengyuan of the South Tang, and also the second year of Tianfu of the Later Jin Dynasty.

954 AD At age of 18, he married Ehuang (Queen Zhou) in 954 AD.

958 AD At age of 22, his first son was born, named Zhong Yu.

959 AD Li Yu was 23 years old in 959 AD when it was the sixth year of the Later Zhou Dynasty's Xiande period.

In September 959 AD, Prince Hongji was dead, Li Yu was bestowed as King Wu instead of King Zheng.

961 AD Li Yu was 25 years old, established as an imperial prince of South Tang. He sat on the throne in capital city Jinling.

His mother bestowed as saint revered queen and Ehuang as Queen. An envoy was sent to report such an inheritage to the Song Dynasty.

His second son was born in 961 AD.

962 AD Li Yu was 26 years old. In March, an envoy was sent to present tribute to the Song Dynasty, and in June and in November, also did the same thing.

963 AD At age of 27, it was the first year of Qiande (imperial "reign title") of the North Song Dynasty.

In March, The Song Armymen quelled the rebellion of Jingnan, and the South-Tang envoy gave a bonus to the Song Dynasty's Army Division.

In November, the Song Dynasty began to change its imperial "reign title" into Qiande.

964 AD At age of his 28, it was the second year of Qiande in the North Song Dynasty.

In March, iron money in cash used to be popular.

In October, his second son Zhongxuan was dead.

In November, Queen Ehuang Zhou was dead. Li Yu wrote <Eulogy to Queen Zhaohui Zhou>.

965 AD At age of his 29. It was the third year of Qiande in the North Song Dynasty.

January, Queen Zhaohui was buried in Yiling Tomb.

April, the Song conquered Kingdom Shu, the South-Tang paid a tribute of 10000-unit silver coins and silk products.

966 AD At age of his 30. It was the fourth year of Qiande in the North Song Dynasty. Emperor Zhao Kuangyin made a decree to ask the South-Han to meet him for discussing current situation together, but failed. Thus the Song decided to fight for the South Han.

968 AD Li Yu was 32 years old. In June, as an envoy, his younger brother, Li Congqian was sent to present tribute to the Song imperial court.

In November, Li Yu married Younger Zhou being bestowed as a queen.

969 AD At age of his 33, hunting in the Green-Dragon Mountain, inspecting the prisoners caught by the Dalisi Supreme Court. Li Yu let all the monks and nuns relieve their hardship.

971 AD At age of his 35, his younger brother was sent to the Song imperial court to bring with the treasures much more than ever before.

In October, as an envoy, his younger brother, Li Congshan was sent to present tribute to the the Song imperial court.

Submitting a written statement to change the state title — South Tang Empire into Riverside South State, and its top leader would be called subordinate monarch instead of emperor.

972 AD At age of his 36. January, a derogatory ceremonial system was drawn that the so-called imperial decree would be changed into teachings.

The South-Tang monarch would wear the violet robe to pay a formal visit to the Song emperor. February, leap year, Li Congshan was kept as an imperial governor of the Song in charge of both civil and military affairs while he was responsible for building Grand Hotel in Bianliang (Kaifeng) in order to receive Li Yu as the South Tang monarch coming to join his surrendered ceremony.

973 AD At age of his 37. Reported to the Song emperor for accepting of conferred dukedom title, the Song did not permit to kill famous general Lin Renzhao.

974 AD At age of his 38. Reported the Song imperial court to ask envoy Li Congshan to return to South-Tang, but being refused and ordered Li Yu to see the Song emperor. Li Yu's refusal caused the Song to attack South Tang in a military way.

975 AD At age of 39. the Song Army was marching onto Jinling city's outside.

In March, the united army force of Wu and Yue was to besiege Changzhou City, then the City-guarded army was surrendered.

In June, Jinling city was besieged by the united army of Song, Wu and Yue. Emperor Zhao Kuangyin warned the South Tang to surrender soon. November 27, Jinling city was occupied. Being captured, Monarch Li Yu with his 4 official and family members in all followed after Song General Cao Bing to go northward to Bianliang. Since then the South Tang regime was dead.

976 AD At age of 40, in January (Chinese lunar calendar), Li Yu was conferred to be Imperial Guard General and Order-Violating Duke of the Song Dynasty. In November, another honorable title, Longxi Nobleman was conferred.

978 AD Li Yu was 42 years old in 978 AD when it was the third year, Taipingxingguo-Period, the North Song Dynasty. July 8, 978 AD, the Song Emperor Zhao Guangyi poisoned Li Yu, and bestowed Li Yu as King Wu. October, 978 AD, Li Yu was buried in Bei-mang-shan Tomb. And later in the same year, his second Queen, Younger Zhou died and was buried in the same tomb.

（2）李煜的墓志铭——《大宋左千牛卫上将军追封吴王陇西公墓志铭》

徐铉 撰写

盛德[1]百世，善继者所以主其祀；圣人无外，善守者不能固其存。盖运历[2]之所推，亦古今之一贯。其有享蕃锡[3]之宠，保克终之美，殊恩饰壤，懿范[4]流光，传之金石，斯[5]不诬矣。

王讳煜，字重光，陇西人也。昔庭坚[6]赞九德，伯阳[7]恢[8]至道，皇天眷佑[9]，锡祚[10]于唐。祖文宗武，世有显德。载祀三百，龟玉沦胥[11]。宗子维城[12]，蕃衍万国。江淮之地，独奉长安。故我显祖，用膺推戴。耀前烈，载光旧吴。二世承基，克广其业。皇宋将启，玄贶[13]冥符[14]。有周开先，太祖历试，威德所及，寰宇将同。故我旧邦，祗畏天命，贬大号以禀朔[15]，献池图[16]而请吏。故得义动元[17]后，风行域中，恩礼有加，绥怀[18]不世[19]。鲁用天王之礼，自越裳[20]钧[21]，存纪侯之国，曾何足贵。王以世嫡嗣服[22]，以古道驭民。钦若[23]彝伦[24]，率循[25]先志。奉蒸尝[26]，恭色养[27]，必以孝；宾大臣，事耆老[28]，必以礼。居处服御[29]必以节，言动施舍必以仁。至于荷全济之恩，谨蕃国之度，勤修九贡[30]，府无虚月；祗奉百役，知无不为。十五年间，天眷弥渥[31]。然而果于自信，怠于周防，西邻起衅，南箕[32]构祸。投杼致慈亲之惑，乞火无里媪之辞。始营因垒之师，终后涂山之会[33]。大祖至仁之举，大赉[34]为怀；录勤王[35]之前效，恢[36]焚谤[37]之广度。位以上将，爵为通侯，待遇如初，宠锡斯厚。今上宣猷[38]大麓[39]，敷惠万方，每侍论思，常存开释。及飞天在运，丽泽推恩，擢进[40]上公之封，仍加掌武[41]之秩。侍从亲礼，勉谕[42]优容。方将度越等彝[43]，登崇名数[44]。

呜呼！阅川无舍，景命不融，太平兴国三年秋七月八日，遘疾薨于京师里第，享年四十有二。皇上抚几兴悼，投瓜轸悲，痛生之不逮。俾殁而加饰，特诏辍朝三日，赠太师，追封吴王，命中使莅葬。凡丧祭所须，皆从官给。及其年冬十月日，葬于河南府某县某乡某里，礼也。夫人郑国夫人[45]周氏，勋旧之族，是生邦媛，肃雍之美，流咏国风。才实女师，言成阃[46]则。子右千牛卫大将军某，襟神俊茂，识度淹通，孝悌自表于天资，才略靡由于师训，日出之学，未易可量。

惟王天骨秀颖，神气清粹，言动有则，容止可观。精究六经，旁综百氏。常以为周孔之道，不可暂离，经国化民，发号施令，造次于是，始终不渝。酷好文辞，多所述作。一游一豫，必颂宣尼[47]。载笑载言，不忘经义。洞晓音律，精别雅郑[48]；穷先王制作之意，审风俗淳薄之原。为文谕之，以续《乐记》。所著文集三十卷，杂说百篇。味其文，知其道矣。至于弧矢[49]之善，笔札之工，天纵多能，必造精绝。本以恻隐之性，仍好竺乾[50]之教。草木不杀，禽鱼咸遂。赏人之善，常若不及；掩人之过，惟恐其闻。以至法不胜奸，威不克爱。以厌兵之俗，当用武之世。孔明罕应变之略，不成近功；偃王[51]躬仁义之行，终于亡国。道有所在，复何愧欤[52]？

呜呼哀哉！二室南峙，三川东注，瞻上阳之宫阙，望北邙之灵树，旁寂寂兮回野，下冥冥兮长暮。寄不朽于金石，庶有[53]传于竹素[54]。其铭曰：

天鉴九德，锡我唐祚[55]。
绵绵瓜瓞[56]，茫茫商土[57]。
裔孙有庆，旧物重睹。
开国承家，疆吴跨楚。
丧乱[58]孔棘[59]，我恤畴依[60]。
圣人既作，我知所归。
终日靡俟[61]，先天不违。
惟藩惟辅，永言固之。
道或污隆[62]，时有险易。
蝇止于棘，虎游于市。
明明大君，宽仁以济。
嘉尔前哲，释兹后至。
亦觐[63]亦见，乃侯乃公。
沐浴元泽，徊翔景风。
如松之茂，如山之崇。
奈何不淑[64]，运极化穷[65]。

旧国疏封[66]，新阡[67]启室。

人谂[68]之谋，卜云其吉。

龙章骥德[69]，兰言[70]玉质。

邈尔何往[71]，此焉终毕。

俨青盖兮祥祥[72]，驱素虬[73]兮迟迟。

即隧路兮徒返，望君门兮永辞。

庶九原[74]之可作，与缑岭[75]兮相期。

斯文于亿载，将乐石[76]兮无亏。

【译注】

李煜墓志铭，即《大宋左千牛卫上将军追封吴王陇西公墓志铭并序》。其出处为徐铉《骑省集·卷二九》。

①盛德：有高尚品德。

②运历：运数，命运。

③蕃锡：（对附属国）恩赐。

④懿范：美好的道德风范。【晋】陆云《赠顾骠骑·有皇》诗："思我懿范，万民来服。"

⑤斯：有"这"（这里，这个），"此""卑贱"等含义。

⑥庭坚：古代相传为高阳氏八个有才德的人之一。详见《左传·文公十八年》"八恺"。一说庭坚即是尧舜时期的狱官皋陶。

⑦伯阳：古贤人。相传为舜七友之一。

⑧恢：使……拓宽。

⑨眷佑：亦作"睠佑"，眷顾佑助。

⑩锡祚：赐福。

⑪龟玉沦胥：象征权力的瑰宝，相与沦胥同付诸东流,如淡淡流水一样消失了（沦胥而逝）。沦胥（lún xǔ）：同"沦滑"，相率牵连；泛指沦陷、沦丧。

⑫宗子维城：“大宗”和“宗子”均指周代贵族中根据血缘关系对族人拥有管辖和处置权的人。原文出于“大邦维屏，大宗维翰。怀德维宁，宗子维城”。（【译文】大国是屏障，大族是栋梁。为政有德国安宁，宗子是城墙。）（翰：栋梁。宗子：嫡姓长子。）

⑬玄贶（xuán kuàng）：上天的赏赐；皇帝的赏赐。

⑭冥符：默契，暗合。

⑮禀朔（bǐng shuò）：奉行正朔。喻臣服。《梁书·武帝纪上》：“浃海宇以驰风，罄轮裳而禀朔。”

⑯池图：护城河图。通“饰”。“池者，缘饰之名，谓其形象水池耳。池与饰通用。这是由于宋代毡面如水池花纹，因而得名池毡。这样的花纹，也只限于宋代。而宋朝恐只限于京都。别的朝代或别的地方，毡被没有这种花纹，‘池’也就不能与‘饰’通假，因为它们没有‘约定俗成’的社会群众基础。”（引自黄现璠著《古书解读初探——黄现璠学术论文选》）

⑰（得义动）元：始也。

⑱绥怀：安抚关切。

⑲不世：不是每代都有的,即非常、非凡。形容功劳极大。《后汉书·隗嚣传》：足下将建伊吕之业,弘不世之功。

⑳越裳：越裳为中国南方古老民族名称。

㉑钧：钧和衡都是量物的工具，借为评量人才之意。

㉒嗣服：继承先人的事业。

㉓钦若：敬顺。《书·尧典》：“乃命羲和，钦若昊天，历象日月。”

㉔彝伦（yí lún）：常理；常道。

㉕率循：遵循；依循。

㉖蒸尝：本指秋冬二祭,后泛指祭祀。

㉗色养：百善孝为先，孝顺父母最高境界是“色养”。（色养：指晚辈孝敬前辈的一种言行最高规范。发自内心、出于虔敬，不可对长者犯以颜色，不可只在表面的给他人“以示孝心”。）

㉘耆老（qí lǎo）：[aged person]六十曰耆，七十曰老，原指六七十岁的老人。

㉙服御：亦作“服驭”。服饰车马器用之类；驾驭车马。

㉚九贡：中国西周王朝的土贡制度。西周时代九贡内容包括：（1）祀贡，（2）嫔贡，（3）器贡，（4）币贡，（5）材贡，（6）货贡，（7）服贡，（8）斿贡，（9）物贡。

㉛弥渥：优待。出自“怜遇弥渥”（宠爱恩遇；怜爱优待）。

㉜南箕：星名。即箕宿。

㉝涂山之会：是中国夏朝建立的标志性事件。涂山位于今天安徽蚌埠怀远县，传说禹建都阳翟（河南禹县）后召集夏和夷的部落首领于涂山，史称涂山之会。

㉞大赉：慷慨赐予。

㉟勤王：指君主制国家中君王有难，而臣下起兵救援君王（皇帝）。

㊱恢：大也，扩大，发扬。

㊲焚谤：销毁谗言。

㊳宣猷：公开说出，散布。

㊴大麓：麓，录也。

㊵擢（zhuó）进：提拔进用。

㊶掌武：唐代太尉的别称。

㊷勉谕：晓喻；劝说。

㊸度越等彝：超越了封建等级制度“常理、法理”。

㊹名数：名分。

㊺郑国夫人：小周后的封号。是暗含耻辱性的封号。（孔子说：“郑声淫。”郑国夫人，也就意味淫荡夫人。暗讽小周后，抢娥皇姐姐的丈夫——李煜。）

㊻阃（kǔn）：门槛，特指城郭的门槛。

㊼宣尼：宣尼即孔子。西汉平帝元始元年（公元1年)追谥孔子为褒成宣尼公，后人称孔子为宣尼。

㊽雅郑：雅乐和郑声。古代儒家以郑声为淫邪之音，因以“雅郑”指正声和淫邪之音。

㊾弧矢：拱顶在拱脚水平线上的高度，不是圆的半径，而是大大小于半径，这个高度

叫作弧矢。

㊿竺乾：天竺，古印度的别称。

51偃王：嬴姓徐氏，名诞。西周时徐国国君。徐国统辖今淮、泗一带。建都徐城（今宿迁市泗洪县）。周穆王末年，徐君偃好行仁义，前来归顺的东夷国家有40多个。

52欤（yú）：文言助词，表示疑问、感叹、反诘等语气。

53庶有："庶有，犹庶类也。"

54竹素：犹竹帛。多指史册、书籍。

55唐祚：大唐的时运、命运。

56瓜瓞（guā dié）：喻子孙繁衍，相继不绝。《诗经·大雅·绵》："绵绵瓜瓞，民之初生，自土沮漆。"

57商土：与乡土比照而言，源于乡土，与城商开始有更多的联系。从乡土中国到商土中国长期以来，中国社会的人口绝大部分居住在乡村，他们黏着在土地上，是土里土气的乡下人；在经济上是小农经济，种地。

58丧乱：死亡祸乱。后多以形容时势或政局动乱。

59孔棘：很紧急；很急迫。《诗经·小雅·采薇》："岂不日戒，玁狁孔棘。"郑玄笺："孔，甚也；棘，急也。"

60畴依：畴，田地。指一田园民歌（标题）。

61靡俟（mǐ sì）：萎靡不振地等待。

62污隆：升与降。常指世道的盛衰或政治的兴替。

63覯（gòu）：字从见，从冓（gōu），本义为撞见，偶然遇见，不期而遇。

64不淑：不善良，不吉利。

65运极化穷：乐极生悲。

66疏封：帝王把土地或爵位分赐给臣子。

67新阡：新筑的墓道。

68谂（shěn）：规谏，劝告。"岂不怀归，是用作歌，将母来谂。"

69骥德：良骥在其德而不在其力。骥不称其力，称其德也。

70兰言：喻指心意相投的言论。

⑪邈尔何往：美妙远景何在。

⑫裶裶（fēi）：衣服长的样子。

⑬素虬（qiú）：亦称“素蚪”，古代传说中的白龙马。

⑭九原：春秋时晋国卿大夫的墓地在九原，因称墓地。

⑮缑岭（gōu lǐng）：即缑氏山。多指修道成仙之处。

⑯乐石：原指可制乐器的石料，因《峄山石刻文》用此石镌刻，后以之泛指碑石。

Epitaph of Li Yu Bestowed as Imperial Guard General, King Wu, Longxi First-Class Nobility, the Song Dynasty Written by Xu Xuan

The noble moral trait would last for hundreds of years, from generation to generation. A good successor would advocate worship. No sage did not to do so. But a conservative successor could hardly keep his morality. According to destiny, all the present and past people would keep to do the same and share the imperial favor as well as everlasting grace bestowed, which would beautify the land to be brilliant as time going on, and that would be transferred and carved on the goldlike stone not to be tarnished.

King Wu, as Li Yu's revered honorary title. Yu was considered as a taboo word, Chongguang as Li Yu's another first name (in ancient times, a person's first name was often used to explain one's first name in meaning). In history, as a wise scholar, Ting Jian advocated the nine-character of virtues, (namely, " be loyal, trustful, respectful, upright, gentle, cooperative, solid, virtuous and obedient" used to describe human morality as good quality). Another ancient scholar, Bo Yang developed such a perfect moral system, and won good care and safeguard from the Heavenly Emperor who blessed the South Tang to make cultural and military achievements with noble morality to hand down from generation to generation.

The ancestry dynasty had established to last 300-year long, but the Sajik seemed to be tortoise shells and pretty jade had been easily broken and fallen into the deep sea. Imperial forefathers and later generations had to defend their cities, meanwhile myriad vassal states established everywhere.

The territory covered the vast domain of Yangtze River and Huai River. As the sovereignty state was once only to worship to Chang'an as the Tang Dynasty's capital city.

Therefore, we should glorify our imperial ancestry and try our best to strengthen it heartily. Let the forefather brilliant and old Tang empire fame-carrying to inherit and develop the two former imperial generations' achievements.

The Song Empire would start in power, being mysteriously blessed and bestowed by the Heaven, which seemed to be the Zhou Dynasty to establish in political power initially. The Song Dynasty founder would borrowed the historical ruling experience in the same way with its authoritative virtues to spread over everywhere. The same thing would happen to all over the universal. Therefore as an old kingdom, it only feared of the heavenly destiny,deliberately to belittle the imperial title, and handed in a fine map to show truly surrendering idea to invite the Song high officials to come, which meant to start a new turning point by means of righteousness. The loyal thanksgiving attitude with official ritual was unmatched. Lu Kingdom used to follow after the Heavenly King's ritual theories to store Yueshang Kingdom's precious treasure in Jihou Kingdom, which seemed to be enough generous.

King Wu inherited predecessors' cause, applying ancient moral theories of Lu Kingdom to guide the people to behave in moral trait, and that reflected ancient forefathers' will.

King Wu dedicated to worship ancestors to respect and obey forefathers with filial piety, and hospitably to treat imperial officials, politely to concern old pals. Both words and deeds were emphasized in polite manners. Be frugal for the King to live and to travel by imperial cart, and benevolent to devote charity to the people. As an affiliated country, it had been grateful to the metropolitan country, and it always kept on abiding concerned laws and often regulating various tributes so that the governmental management office was always busy in each month in order to respectfully offer all kinds of laboring products without any hesitation.

For fifteen years, the Heavenly Dynasty had bestowed the South Tang a great favor. However, it was once so self-convinced that it could hardly effectively prepare to defend and protect itself. Therefore, the western and southern neighboring countries stirred up trouble on purpose to surround and occupy its territory. As a saying goes, putting down the loom might let mother uneasy. Not to flatter a cook could not seek for a cooking fire. At first its army only depended on barracks fortress of the city, and then it had eventually to be helpless to join "Mount Tushan Union" secretly planned by Great Yu King (an ancient well-known wise and powerful heroic king).

The Song-Dynasty founder emperor was extremely benevolent with his generous mind, considering King Wu's loyalty ago, and widely developing burning defamation spirit so as to confer him as a great general and duke title, still treated him as an previous monarch with top treat.

At present time, King Wu need widely collect opinions and silently to seal his bestowed benefits everywhere. Whenever something theoretical to discuss, it was necessary to explain in a public way. And being super fate was still to depend on fate and mutual help, which meant two merging swamps to be full and charming. A former monarch from the first-class nobility was still politely safeguarded by an imperial high guard official , which meant the loser would not lose face so that would surpass the feudal hierarchy to share imperial noble fame.

Alas! On the vast plain, no home could be seen. The natural scenery was not agreeable with King Wu's doom, who met unexpectedly disease to die at his age of 42, on July 8, autumn, in the Taipingxingguo Dynasty period, in a Luxury Apartment of the capital city. The Song Dynasty emperor expressed himself deeply for the dead sad mourning. The dead was dressed up in a funeral way. The Song imperial court would cease working for three days. The dead was awarded as an honorary title King Wu and Taishi (Great Master). The funeral officials were in charge of burying affairs. All the funeral expenses would be paid by the imperial court.

And the funeral ceremony would be held on some month, some day, some year in a village, a county, Henan Province, King Wu's Queen Zhou was born beautifully in a meritorious family. She was solemn and optimistic with grace and dignity. Her style reflected her motherland style. She was talented like a model teacher speaking not to violate any morality.

King Wu's son bestowed as an ox-symbolic mighty Guard General, an open-minded handsome and unrestrained guy with genius nature and rich knowledge. His Filial Piety originated from his innate character qualifications in natural language. His talent and strategy did not come from teachers' teaching. In the future, his intelligent and creative ability would be impossible to easily estimate.

Only King Wu's mind was wonderfully excellent in noble spirits and he could speak reasonably. It's worth to watch his regulating behavior. King Wu mastered Six–Classic-Books, and wrote over one-hundred classic articles. As a rule, he always followed the ancient Zhou Dynasty and scholarly Confucian theories and teachings to manage the country, educate the people and issue orders. Even though he was busy, he would not forget benevolent doctrine and also wrote more literary and poetic works. Even in a sightseeing tour, still he would like to express himself through poetry and quotations from classic books. He was speaking while smiling. He did not forget classic-writing ideas. Being good in music sense and poetic rhyme, he was elegant but not vulgar.

Be in exhaustive way to take careful consideration of ancient wise kings' creative intent try to understand the original reason to be good or evil in common customs. It was necessary to discuss before writing any article. And then it would be possible continuously to enrich such an ancient book "Music-Writing Notes" and 30 volumes of "Collected Works" as well as 100 articles entitled "Miscellaneous Essays". Writings mirror the writer, from which readers could understand his theories. King Wu was good at bow-throwing skills, good at calligraphy. Still he was versatile with gifted talent and still to study hard to seek for absolutely excellent progress.

With strong compassion of nature, he believed in Buddha and never to kill living birds or fish and always was used to appreciate others' merits and strong points. Be sure to help others in time and try to cover their shortcomings and errors to protect their fame and reputation.

Thus alone the lawful way can not punish evil and mischief, yet all the lawful rules could not excite human affectionate love and benevolence. When the common customs were to disgust war, the world had been under the military power threatening. As an ancient wise man, Kong Ming lacked flexible response of strategy, therefore he won no more military achievements in the short period of time. King Yan bent his body and exhausted his energy to practice his benevolence and righteousness administration, but ultimately his kingdom was subjugated. Nowadays some rulers still look gentlemanly; they should not be ashamed to be blamed.

Alas! The couple of grave located to face the southern peaks, three rivers flowing toward east, looking up at the sunny palace and watching the fairy trees of the North Mang. Oh, outside, the vast field was lonely voicelessly; under the sky, the long twilight seemed deeper and deeper. Let the epitaph stone be immortal; let everything moral be recorded in books.

The epitaph inscribed like this:

The Heaven mirrors the nine-character virtues,
Bestowing the South Tang throne and happiness.

A long long vine with sweet melons, one after another,
The agrestic land once expanding vaster and vaster.

The later generation would feel fortunate in celebration,
They could not help seeing the native land again.

The Sajik established to inherit from our own home,
Our domain had crossed from Wu to Chu Kingdom.

The funeral ceremony was in urgent disorder,
Emperor's predestined song we sympathized.

The wise man pointed the goal,
We could know where to go.

The King slouching to wait for his fate all day long,
The Sajik's will was not violated, but to go on.

Only as an affiliated and vassal kingdom,
The Sajik would be affirmed to stand firm.

Morality and justice might rise or fall,
The situation would go dangerous or well.

Flying flies rested in the bush thorn,
Escaping tigers wandered in the town.

Grand monarch behaved in a magnanimous style,
With benevolence to help the affiliated or the vassal.

To eulogize great thinkers of the past,
Whereas to release annoyance in heart.

Reuniting unexpectedly while staring mutually,
Duke title plus noble title awarded honorably.

As if swimming in the mysterious pond,
The soul might wander in scenic wind.

Like green pines, standing proudly,
Like lofty mountains, lying voicelessly.

No avail to change the dark dynasty,
Poverty originated from no good destiny.

Officials awarded as a higher title in the old kingdom,
They would apply the distributed land to begin new room.

One would know how to plan a scheme,
That meant he could foretell lucky doom.

Writing like a dragon skillfully flying and dancing,
Orchid-symbolic gentle talk like jewelry charming.

Where you are going far far away,
Here is the final place on the fairy way.

Oh, see casket's long long cover in blue solemnly,
Oh, move your coffin of dragonlike body slowly.

Alas, stopping at the grave site, unable to be back again,
Alas, watching the door shut, you are no longer seen.

Perhaps, in Jiuyuan Cemetery, the death might be survival,
Look forward to seeing the Fairy Mountain's immortal.

The graceful epitaph would ever last,
The inscription stone would be perfect.

【徐铉简介】

徐铉（916~991），五代宋初文学家、书法家。字鼎臣，广陵（今江苏扬州）人，南唐翰林学士、吏部尚书，后随李煜归宋，官至散骑常侍，世称徐骑省。曾受诏与句中正等校定《说文解字》。与韩熙载齐名，江东谓之“韩徐”。

有诗作流传于世。现选译一首，请读者欣赏徐铉这首严肃的诗作：

送王四十五归东都①

海内兵方起②，离筵泪易垂。

怜③君负米④去，惜此落花时。

想忆看来信⑤，相宽指后期⑥。

殷勤⑦手中柳，此是向南枝。

【译注】

①王四十五：未知其名，“四十五”是在兄弟（包括从兄弟）中的排行。东都：指江都府——扬州。五代南唐都江宁府，即今日南京，称西都，遂把五代吴的旧都江都府称为东都。

②海内兵方起：公元960年，赵匡胤夺取后周政权建立宋王朝后，先后用兵攻破荆南、后蜀、南汉等，南唐亦已朝不虑夕。

③怜：即爱。

④负米：《孔子家语·致思》：“子路见孔子曰：‘由也，事二亲之时，常食藜藿之实，为亲负米百里之外。’”后把孝养父母称作“负米”。

⑤想忆：指别后思念。看来信：一作“望来信”。

⑥后期：指后会之期。

⑦殷勤：情意恳切。

[A Brief Introduction to Xu Xuan]

Xu Xuan (916-991) was the Song Dynasty writer and calligrapher. He styled himself Dingchen. Guangling (now Yangzhou) was his birthplace. As a scholar in the South Tang Imperial Academy, he was appointed as Minister of the State Personnel Ministry. Following Li Yu to return to the Song Dynasty court, he was appointed as an emperor attendant being called Xu Cross-riding-province supervisor, and was invited to be a chief editor for checking an authoritative Dictionary entitled "Talking texts and explaining single words". He was as famous as another imperial high official Han Xizai.

Xu Xuan had poems spreading in the world. Now let me select one of his poems for readers to appreciate.

Send off King 45 to return to Yangzhou

Soldiers just went to the front of the domestic war,
Tears easily were to shed in the farewell dinner.
I would sympathize to your filial piety to return,
When it is the season that blooming flowers wane.
My good memories attract me to see your letter,
My comfort is to look forward to seeing you later.
I hold a weeping willow twig in my hand to you,
It was a lovely twig of the south-direction willow.

（3）南唐简介（937~975）

南唐（937~975年）是五代十国之一，定都金陵(今南京)，历时39年，有先主李昪、中主李璟和后主李煜三位帝王。南唐一朝，最盛时幅员35州，大约地跨今江西全省及安徽、江苏、福建和湖北、湖南等省的一部分。人口约五百万。南唐三世，经济发达，文化繁荣，使得江淮地区在五代乱世中“比年丰稔，兵食有余”，为中国南方的经济开发做出了重大贡献。南唐国也因此成为中国历史上重要的政权之一。但因资料和遗迹极少，并未得到社会和学术界的足够重视。

The South Tang Dynasty (937~975)

The South Tang Dynasty (937~975), which lasted 39 years, was one of the Five Dynasties with Ten Kingdoms. Its capital city was Jinling (Nanking). There had been three emperors to reign the whole period of South Tang. The first monarch was Li Bian, the second was Li Jing and the last was Li Yu. On its heyday, South Tang covered 35 states, approximately across the whole part of Jiangxi province, a few parts of Anhui, Jiangsu, Fujian and Hubei, Hunan and other provinces. It had over five-million people. During the South Tang's Three Reigns, its economy developed, culture was in prosperity, making Jiang-Huai vast region get good harvest every year and have grain enough to support military army in the disorder period of China's Five Dynasties. Its economic development of the South China made a significant contribution. The South Tang had thus become an important political power in China's history. But with very little information and relics, it has not been paid enough attention in the social and academic circles.